Prestel M

Folkwang Museum
Learning by Seeing

Prestel

Munich · Berlin · London · New York

KARL ERNST OSTHAUS
∗1874 Hagen   †1921 Merano

Foreword

The Folkwang Museum is one of Germany's most renowned art museums, with an outstanding collection of 19th century paintings and sculpture, classic modernism, post-1945 art, and photography. The strong point of the collection is German and French painting since 1800. The forerunners of modernism—Cézanne, Gauguin and Van Gogh—feature with major paintings, but there are also masterpieces by German Romantics Caspar David Friedrich and C. G. Carus and French artists Courbet, Daumier, Monet and Renoir.

Numerous German Expressionist paintings by the Die Brücke group match the work of the Blauer Reiter artists in quality. Notable strengths of the post-1945 collection include German Informel and American Colour Field paintings, with outstanding examples by Barnett Newman, Ad Reinhardt, Mark Rothko and Frank Stella. Large-format paintings by Georg Baselitz, Anselm Kiefer, Sigmar Polke and Per Kirkeby complete the picture. In recent times, greater attention has been paid to acquiring sculptures, installations and large-format photographs by contemporary artists.

In 1979, the Folkwangschule für Gestaltung's study collection built up by Otto Steinert was integrated into the Folkwang Museum, and has existed as a separate department since then. The collection of paintings and sculptures includes about 800 works, the Graphic Art Collection about 12,000 works on paper, and the Photographic Collection over 50,000 photographs and several artists' estates.

In 2005, the collection was completely reorganised and rehung. Classic modernist drawings, watercolours and graphic works have now found a place alongside the paintings. European and non-European applied art from ancient times to the 19th century can now be seen side by side with classic modernist sculptures and contemporary art. This juxtaposition respects the intentions of both museum founder Karl Ernst Osthaus in Hagen and the first museum director in Essen, Ernst Gosebruch. It is how the collection was arranged originally. From 1902 to 1933 it formed a great synthesis of world art ranging from ancient Iran, ancient Egypt, the Far East, medieval Europe and Africa to the contemporary world. In an age of increasing globalisation and intercultural relations, that approach seems more topical than ever.

The recent rehang takes the search for common features of world cultures and their differences into account, as far as the works in the collections allow. The present guide to the collection attempts to facilitate in an appropriate fashion this encounter between items that are disparate and yet related to each other. Each of the double page spreads in 'learning by seeing' describes a grouping that brings works—over and above their differences in space, time and genre—into dialogue with each other, inviting readers to practise making comparisons as they look, and as they look, to understand.

Hubertus Gassner
DIRECTOR, FOLKWANG MUSEUM

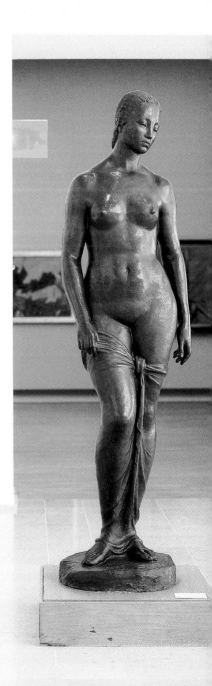

Folkwang Museum, Hagen
Entrance hall, c. 1907

The Folkwang Museum.
Origins and the present

The Folkwang Museum would have been 100 years old on 19 July 2002. It was opened in 1902 by the still youthful collector and art patron Karl Ernst Osthaus (1874–1921) in the Westphalian industrial town of Hagen, as a private museum open to the public. It can rightly be seen as the oldest museum of modern art in Europe and America. This museum, which was the first German collection to acquire a painting by Gauguin and the first to show works by Vincent van Gogh and Henri Matisse, pointed the way forward for many institutions founded later.

In 1920, shortly before the death of its dedicated and far-sighted founder, art critic Franz Servaes wrote a paean of praise to his epoch-making initiative in the *Jahrbuch der jungen Kunst*: 'No art collection organised for the benefit of the public in the whole territory of the German Reich has played a more powerful pioneering role than this private establishment, which arose as much from enlightened discernment and sheer daring as from pure, selfless enthusiasm.'

And it was not only as a museum of modern art that Osthaus's Folkwang Museum was a pioneer. As a collector, he also took far more risks than contemporaries in Germany who had like him dedicated themselves to collecting modern art from around 1900 on. Most collectors at that time tended to acquire works that were over 20 years old, but even in the first decade of the 20th century Karl Ernst Osthaus moved on from French Post-Impressionism to the Fauvism of artists such as Henri Matisse and Georges Braque and German Expressionists of the Brücke and Blauer Reiter groups. By buying straight from young progressive artists' studios, Osthaus became a model for German collectors who came after him. But in contrast with some of the latter, financial constraints during and after the First World War meant that Karl Ernst Osthaus was unable to add Cubists to his collection of French Fauves and German Expressionists.

In 1900, Osthaus made his first contact with Henry van de Velde, the Belgian Art Nouveau painter, graphic artist and architect. He wrote to him on 26th April: 'I am setting up a museum which aims to create an interest in modern art in our art-forsaken industrial area on the Ruhr. As the sole owner of my institution, I am in the happy position of not having to take any prejudices into account and therefore wish to create an attractive building based entirely on modern requirements and— as far as my means will permit—an exemplary one. It is the desire to ensure your esteemed co-operation in this project that brings me to

Brussels. In the hope that your interest will by awakened by my enterprise, I remain most respectfully yours, Karl Ernst Osthaus.'

Van de Velde was interested in the proposal, and when Osthaus visited him in Brussels in May 1900 he managed to persuade the Flemish artist to commit himself to the project. But Van de Velde did not come to Hagen simply to take over the interior decoration of the museum building, which was already complete as a shell, and offset his predecessor's Renaissance Revival façade with Art Nouveau architecture and interior furnishings. The architect and graphic artist also designed furniture, jewellery, silver, clothes and tableware for Osthaus and his wife Gertrud, and became his client's most important adviser on purchasing works of modern and contemporary art. It is first and foremost to Van de Velde's credit that Osthaus rapidly familiarised himself with the most recent artistic movements in Belgium, the Netherlands and above all France, and got in touch with art dealers Ambroise Vollard in France and Paul Cassirer in Berlin. Van de Velde influenced Osthaus's acquisitions significantly, if we bear in mind that as a collector Osthaus had hitherto specialised in 19th century German paintings of the Düsseldorf school of artists and only turned to purchasing international modernism under the Flemish artist's influence, so that within a very short time he had acquired the present showpieces in the Folkwang collection.

Osthaus originally planned the museum as a 'scientific institution', as he called it. But the telegram to Van de Velde already makes clear his far-reaching decision to use the building already under construction to win over the 'art-forsaken' Bergisches Land and Ruhr areas to modern art as well. He had come by the financial resources for building the museum and for his various collections by way of a substantial legacy from his grandfather. Suddenly the student who had read philosophy, literature and art history in Munich, Berlin (under Grimm and Curtius), Strasbourg (Dehio) and finally Vienna was 'in a position to put into practice ideas that had had exercised me greatly over the years. They were aimed at raising the industrial west culturally—I had experienced its development and had a keen sense of its spiritual neglect. My intention was to found various institutions intended to serve scientific and cultural purposes,' he wrote.

In 1889, excursions with an entomologist took the youthful Osthaus into the Atlas Mountains and the Sahara, which aroused his interest in Islamic culture. Studies of art history and more travel enabled him to extend his newly acquired interest in oriental and Islamic culture. Osthaus returned to Hagen from these excursions with numerous collectors' pieces such as woven textiles, embroidery, carpets, coins, weapons and pottery, and looked for a suitable place to put them on show. When the museum he had planned in Hagen for these and other natural history collections finally opened in July 1902, it included—in the museum founder's own words— 'three independent departments: a gallery for works of modern art, a collection of historical [European and non-European—*author's note*] applied art and—the scientific objects for which it was built.'

The three different areas of collection were distributed over the three storeys of the new museum building according to content: the natural history collection was accommodated in the basement, including among other things 45,000 beetles and 7,000 butterflies. Osthaus saw the aesthetic properties of natural historical specimens like these as a starting-point for all design in art and applied art. He called an article published in the year the museum opened *Colour harmonies in nature*. On the ground floor above this 'natural basis' for the art forms designed by human hand was the collection of applied art products, and then on the first floor the presentation of art in a narrower sense.

Thus arranged in three levels and intended to provide a kind of microcosm of all spheres of the aesthetic manifestations of beauty in nature, man-made artefacts and 'free art', the museum acquired an architectural and spiritual centrepiece in 1906 in the form of a fountain designed by George Minne, with five identical marble figures of boys. It is now in the Folkwang Museum in Essen. Osthaus commissioned it from the Belgian sculptor in 1905 at Van de Velde's suggestion, and it was placed in the lobby of the Hagen museum in the following year beneath a skylight with a circular wooden balustrade designed by the architect. Toplighting from this 'crown' streams down on to the 'Fountain of Youth', illuminating the naked, marble-white figures of boys bending over the surface of the water.

The founder himself put the symbolic significance of this source of water in the centre of the museum into words as early as 1904: 'I feel that museums should in general not be oases in the desert of our modern cities, but a cool spring, whose waves purify the whole of life and flow refreshingly over it.' Thus the central fountain with figures and with it the museum itself became a source of life, assigned the task of renewing society fundamentally through the creative energies of art, purging it of all the tedium of soulless and mechanical routine, mind-numbing work and superfluous conventions.

The name 'Folkwang', which Osthaus chose for his museum, comes from the ancient Nordic myth of the *Edda*, which was to become the 'bible' of the turn-of-the-century German *Jugendbewegung* in its search for the 'new man'. Although the name also alludes to the museum's public educational function (*Volksbildung*), also suggesting thereby a public hall (*Volkshalle*), 'Folkwang' meant above all the palace of the Nordic-Germanic fertility goddess Freya, who was also the patroness of the arts, embodying both the beauty of art and a fertile and creative life. The Folkwang was intended not just to educate the people or even as a place of light entertainment. It was also intended to celebrate the unity of art and life, in other words it was to heighten and intensify life by aestheticising it. But only an élite dreams this dream of a higher life. Even in 1919, when all the old values seemed to have lost their currency after the war and Osthaus himself welcomed the Republic by working on the revolutionary-minded workers' art council, unlike most council members he wanted this to be perceived not so much in terms of workers' democracy as 'in the spirit of a council of intellectual leaders'.

The far-reaching task of 'popular education' destined for the Folkwang Museum owed much to the ideas and projects for reforming life in general that were extraordinarily popular in Germany at the turn of the century as a result of rapid industrialisation and urbanisation. They found an outlet in the reform movements that Osthaus actively supported, which advocated building garden cities, breathing new life into the applied arts, new forms of physical hygiene and care, rhythmic gymnastics and expressive dance, and also new types of school. The founding of the Folkwang Museum and the Deutscher Werkbund, among whose initiators and most active members Osthaus was, were manifestations of the same ideas.

The significance and function of the natural history collection decreased as the emphasis shifted to the museum's aesthetic educational duties, while European and non-European applied art acquired a status equal to that of free art. The description of the collections and their display in the Folkwang Museum in Hagen, probably written by Osthaus himself before 1916, conveys an idea of the central importance the co-founder of the Deutscher Werkbund and forerunner of the Weimar Bauhaus accorded to the reciprocal influence of international applied art products and masterpieces of high European art in his collection.

Around 1916, the natural history collection in the basement was replaced by Islamic art, furniture, carpets, fabrics and metalwork, and also Moorish and early oriental ceramics. On the ground floor were ancient Egyptian bronze and stone equipment, Phoenician glassware, Greek terracotta and bronze, gold jewellery, a marble figure from the time of Praxiteles, early Germanic art, medieval crucifixes, ecclesiastical vestments and manuscripts, and also printed graphics by Dürer and Goya. Separate rooms showed furniture, tapestries and small craft items from the Italian and German Renaissance, and also Baroque furniture and sculpture from North and South Germany, Italy and Spain, plus faïence and Delft tiles. Sculpture, by Constantin Meunier and George Minne among others, stood in the vestibule and on the walls hung paintings by Maurice Denis, Bernard, Thorn-Prikker and Hodler. There were coins and medals on the stairs and in the stairwell, but also copperplate engravings by Rembrandt and Dürer along with

Museum Folkwang Hagen
Gemäldegalerie nach Westen, um 1916

drawings by Matisse and Van Gogh, plus Venetian, Spanish and Bohemian glass. This mixture of aesthetically arranged genres and periods continued cheerfully in the upper storey, even though here, in the picture gallery at least, the main feature was the modern art collection. But here too there were corner cupboards filled with 18th century porcelain, and also lace, fans and women's jewellery of the same period. Gauguin's magnificent painting *Barbarian Tales* was to be admired alongside a temple image from Bali, various sculptures from Egypt, Korea and Ceylon and a Romanesque St. John from Bavaria. Anselm Feuerbach's painting of *Orpheus and Eurydice* hung in another room along with Gauguin's *Kelp Harvesters*, stone sculptures from Korea and a wooden sculpture by George Minne.

Such examples could be continued. They demonstrated in the most striking way Osthaus's idea of a living museum that gives art back to life by suspending all historical and geographical boundaries and arranging the natural history, applied art and free art collections neither chronologically nor art-historically nor according to countries or schools, but in freely combined contrasts and correspondences that allow the inner life and expressive force of the individual works to make a powerful impact as a more intense experience.

As early as 1912 Osthaus was calling the applied and free art 'works by primitive peoples ... absolutely modern' because of their 'technical limitations and genuineness'. Even though numerous avant-garde artists and art theorists, from Cubism and Fauvism to the Brücke Expressionists and the Blauer Reiter, shared these views about the 'modernity' of so-called primitive art, including African tribal art, he was pretty well alone in this view among art historians and the staff of art galleries. Obviously Karl Ernst Osthaus was the first person to dare to document these formal analogies and inner relationships between African or Oceanic art and modern art in a museum as well, and to express and demonstrate visually this hypothesis of the partial spiritual affinity between their creators, and to do that not only in writing or in artists' studios and secluded private collections, but completely in the public eye.

After the enthusiasm of the Cubists and Fauvists in Paris for 'negro art' had brought about its aesthetic rediscovery and re-evaluation from 1906 on, it was taken up by the Brücke artists in Dresden and the Blauer Reiter in Munich. The interest of these two artists' groups in the Hagen Folkwang Museum was reciprocated unequivocally by Osthaus, despite their youth and the provocatively innovative quality of their work. Their common search for the roots of modern art and culture and enthusiasm for 'primitive' art must have been a crucial factor in these mutual demonstrations of sympathy.

As early as December 1906, Erich Heckel, representing the Brücke artists, wrote to Osthaus that the 'modern, and for us exemplary establishment and artistic direction of the Folkwang Museum' had led them to wish 'to be able to arrange an exhibition of our work in the beautiful galleries of this first and at present only modern museum, under your esteemed direction.'

Since the museum had put on the first Van Gogh exhibition in a German museum as early as 1905 and a smaller Ferdinand Hodler exhibition, and then its first Emil Nolde and Edward Munch exhibitions in the following year, it made complete sense to present the most recent exponents of expressive tendencies in contemporary art. Osthaus immediately accepted the Brücke artists' proposal. Their works were shown at the Folkwang in Hagen in summer 1907, and the group had another exhibition there three years later. Osthaus as a patron was

Folkwang Hagen, post-1914,
Asiatic Cabinet

to remain committed to Ernst Ludwig Kirchner in particular until he died in 1921. In gratitude, the artist kept up his links with the Folkwang Museum in Essen even after that date.

Consistent commitment to contemporary art, but above all the combination of old and young, of modern European and non-European 'primitive' art, made the Folkwang Museum attractive not only to the Brücke artists but also to the members of the Blauer Reiter. From 1909 to 1913, Vassily Kandinsky, August Macke, Franz Marc and Gabriele Münter kept up a lively correspondence with Karl Ernst Osthaus.

On his first visit to the Folkwang Museum in 1908, August Macke was '*jeck* (infatuated), as they say here' when he saw the 'exceptionally beautiful collection' with the 'best modernists', combined with 'old things, a lot of Egyptian, Greek, Indian, Gothic and Italian.' Two large-scale one-man shows of Kandinsky and Yavlensky were put on at the Folkwang Museum in 1909, and in November 1911 came a solo exhibition of Franz Marc, from whom Osthaus acquired the major work *The Red Horses*. Marc expressed his thanks by letter on 2nd December 1911 and considered himself 'happy ... to know that there is a work by me in your wonderful museum.' He reported to Osthaus in the same letter that Kandinsky, Gabriele Münter and he had just resigned from the Neue Künstlervereinigung München, with which Osthaus had been negotiating about an exhibition for some time, and they now intended to arrange their own exhibitions as the 'editorial board of the Blauer Reiter Almanac'. The first of these Blauer Reiter exhibitions was also offered to the Folkwang Museum as the first touring venue, as Marc and Kandinsky had high hopes of Osthaus.

In his letter offering it to the museum, Franz Marc identified the particular idea behind this first Blauer Reiter exhibition: 'The basic thought is to allow the enormous differences between the pictures to show that there is no programme and no one-sided direction in art, but that everything really artistic and profound can stand and survive side by side; we have placed the strongest possible contrasts in this exhibition side by side—Henri Rousseau ... alongside Delaunay, Kandinsky and me...We would like to show this exhibition ... in your museum as well, as its very nature provided a model for our train of thought.'

The first Blauer Reiter exhibition took place in Hagen in July 1912, after appearing at other venues. The juxtaposition of different forms of style and expression, the naïve realism of Henri Rousseau beside Kandinsky's intellectual abstraction, which could only be implemented in the sphere of contemporary art in the Blauer Reiter exhibition, was modelled, as Franz Marc rightly remarked, on Osthaus's contrasting combinations and corresponding constellations of works of art from all eras and parts of the world. For years, the Folkwang Museum in Hagen had been putting into practice in its exhibition policy something that the 'manifesto' of modern art in Germany, the Blauer Reiter Almanac, proclaimed only on publication in January 1912, in the form of double-page pictorial montages.

For their comparisons using pairs of similar or dissimilar pictures, the editors of the almanac, Franz Marc and Vassily Kandinsky, juxta-posed avant-garde and popular pictures, among other combinations. Using a double-page spread in each case, the almanac linked very recent paintings with the products of magic cults, or totem figures from ethnographic collections with archaic sculptures from antiquity, in just the same way as the Folkwang Museum.

'The urge to unite the psychically related [has] leapt over epochs and countries and history,' is how Gertrud Osthaus, who perhaps even more than her husband had a feeling for the special features of an individual work of art, summed up the sense of art that motivated the way her husband designed his exhibitions, combining things according to contrast and correspondence. This 'urge to unite' in the context of a museum exhibition showing quite different works is based on the assumption that the contrasts between the works are merely superficial, and that they are closely related inwardly and psychically. Karl Ernst Osthaus's fundamental concern was to identify the single uniform instinct or urge in nature and human culture to endow things with form, an urge that prevails in all things, however different or contrasting they may seem. And he shared this wish with the Blauer Reiter artists and the double-image strategy they used in their manifesto-like almanac.

This abundance of differently designed forms is a manifestation of a single universal artistic urge, which shows itself in nature as well as in the artefacts and works of art created by human hands. Both Osthaus and the Blauer Reiter artists sought evidence of such a creative will above all in peripheral areas of art—rather in folk and applied art, non-European art and children's art than in the high art of classical antiquity, cathedral Gothic or the canons of the Renaissance, whose formal language was mined out by Historicism before the turn of the century. Osthaus rejected revivalism in the form of the Neo-Renaissance façade of his museum and handed the interior design of the museum over to the innovator Van de Velde, who had shaken off all historical styles. Contemporaries were certainly not aware at first how much the latter in his turn had forged a new style embracing everything from teacups and dresses to architecture and town planning.

Osthaus himself defined his own ambition—shared with the Art Nouveau artists and kindred spirits in the Werkbund—for external and internal unity in all things and manifestations including art, in the midst of a world splintered by industrial capitalism and metropolises remote from nature, as 'the essence of the new German art, which is directed not so much at making individual commercial products as at reshaping the whole of life … —a life entirely transformed in the home and society, the bustle of the streets, women's clothes and the rhythm of games and dances.'

If we ask ourselves what the works Osthaus bought for his museum have in common, the best answer is to be found in the collector's own foreword to the catalogue of his art holdings. The lines about his programmatic intentions and objectives close with the declaration:

'The task it [i.e. modern art, *author's note*] faces, and to which the museum has dedicated itself, is to permeate the whole of life with rhythm and beauty.'

Permeating the designed surface of pictures with rhythmical, continuous figures and compositions, the rhythmic articulation and proportioning of sculptures, the rhythms in the patterns and textures of applied art and finally the rhythmic structure of the buildings and architectural elements with the rhythmic flow of architectural ornament became key ideas in Osthaus's aesthetic approach, and a criterion of quality for the works he collected and the projects he funded.

Van de Velde's influence on the formation of Osthaus's taste may also have been responsible for the fact that the latter, unlike most of his contemporaries who were active as major collectors, was scarcely ever able to summon up any enthusiasm for Impressionism. Osthaus always preferred the unifying, rhythmically integrating power of the neo-Impressionism of artists like Gauguin, Van Gogh and Cézanne, but also the rhythmic movement in Art Nouveau, Fauvism and Expressionism to Impressionism's tendency to dissolve pictorial form and the subject of the picture.

Osthaus was scarcely any different from contemporary artists and art theorists of modernism, starting with exponents of the emphatically rhythmic style of Art Nouveau, down to the Cubists, Fauvists, Expressionists and Constructivists, in the fundamental importance he accorded to rhythm as the vehicle of all beauty both in the various art genres and architecture and in nature and human life. In Germany in particular, but throughout Europe and in America as well, concepts of various kinds of rhythm had been finding their way into all spheres of culture at least since the turn of the century. The perception and creative manipulation of rhythm played a central role from high art down to the numerous projects for reforming life in general, from the exact sciences and the humanities, including art history and art psychology, down to the esoteric theories in vogue at the time.

The great reformer, more than most of his contemporaries, had not just sung the praises of the beauty of rhythmic movements as a living counter-force to the harmful consequences of industry that had had such a conspicuous impact in his home region, but had also made it visible in his practical deeds and shown it to its best advantage in a way that was accessible to all. Osthaus devoted himself to more than just the renewal of fine art, applied art and architecture. His wide range of interests also included commitment to the body and life reform movement. Around 1910 he forged plans to found a garden city in which the Swiss dance teacher Emil Jaques-Dalcrose was to set up a school of dance and gymnastics. The Swiss dancer is considered to be the inventor of Rhythmic Gymnastics, which became the basis of expressive dance and fundamentally reformed physical education methods. Osthaus tried to persuade important exponents of Rhythmic Gymnastics such as Jaques-Dalcrose, Russian dancer Aleksandr Sakharov, who was associated with the Blauer Reiter circle, and Elizabeth Duncan's Darmstadt dance school to commit themselves to Hagen on a long-term basis. When these efforts failed, he made a last attempt in 1919-1920 to realise his comprehensive life reform project in the sphere of educational reform by founding an experimental school based on an aesthetic education embracing art, body and soul. But this school project, planned on a Utopian scale with the architect Bruno Taut, with a programme also including a key role for free intellectual development, was short-lived. Only a year later, in March 1921, its intellectual and financial promoter died.

The death of Karl Ernst Osthaus meant that the elements of the network of Folkwang schemes that he had created in 20 years of ceaseless striving for beauty disintegrated all too rapidly into its component parts. The post-war period, with its social and financial hardships, had not proved at all a good environment for Osthaus's great vision of making 'beauty the dominant force in life again'. Everything he had built up in Hagen between 1901 and 1921 fell apart more quickly than it had been built. The Folkwang Museum's collection was sold to Essen in the year he died, while the highly successful arts and crafts museum he founded in 1910 (Deutsches Museum für Kunst in Handel und Gewerbe) was also closed down, its valuable collection passing to the Kaiser Wilhelm Museum in Krefeld. After Osthaus's death the Folkwang Museum was sold to the Essen Folkwang Museum Association, specially created by citizens and companies in 1921 to acquire the collection. It is due to the association's initiative that the outstanding collection from Hagen was kept together in the long term, unlike virtually any other of the important early, private collections in Germany, and is still available and open to the public.

It also proved possible to sustain and successfully continue in Essen in the twenties and early thirties the Hagen Folkwang Museum's pioneering role as the first museum of modern art thanks to a focused exhibition programme and new acquisitions by museum director Dr. Ernst Gosebruch, a friend of Osthaus. But once the museum was detached from the wide-ranging context established by Osthaus, it became a different institution. The Essen purchasers scarcely looked on the collection in the context of the widely cast, life-reforming network set up by Karl Ernst Osthaus. They saw it as a collection of eminently important works of art whose value that was by then for the most part beyond question. As Michael Fehr puts it, the collection 'had to be retained for the Ruhr coal district. To sum up: after its sale, the Folkwang Museum in Hagen was seen as a historical phenomenon and part of another tradition, that of the Folkwang Museum in Essen, for whose development the Hagen roots increasingly lost their significance.'

The ninty-nine paintings and forty-three sculptures taken over from Hagen, as well as the numerous drawings, graphic works and the applied art pieces, fitted in with the municipal art museum's considerable holdings, which complemented Osthaus's collection very well. The Essen museum had been in existence since 1906, and directed by Ernst Gosebruch since 1909. After the two collections had been put together with great sensitivity by Gosebruch, the new Folkwang Museum opened its doors in 1929 in the two Goldschmidt villas in Essen, on the site where the new museum buildings dating from 1959 and 1982 still stand. Certainly there have been considerable and regrettable losses of important works from Osthaus's former collection among the current museum holdings. The collector himself found it necessary to sell some masterpieces, or exchange them for other works, in his own lifetime because of financial difficulties. But above all the museum was so excessively plundered by the Nazis that it existed only as a torso after the Second World War.

The Folkwang Museum, still called 'the most beautiful museum in the world' in America in 1933, fell victim just a year later to the ideological hate campaign against allegedly 'un-German and degenerate art', leading in 1937 to the confiscation of 'decadent German art since 1910' (as Goebbels's decree described it). For Essen, it meant the painful loss of over 1,400 works.

But intelligent and far-sighted purchasing policies by the two museum directors who followed Gosebruch, Heinz Köhn and Paul Vogt, made it possible to close some painful gaps in the fifties and sixties by means of re-acquisitions and purchases comparable to the works that had been lost. In the seventies, they also expanded the collection of painting and sculptures to include contemporary art in such a way that the range of works awaiting the visitor is more extensive today than ever before.

But the collection as a whole has still awaits rehanging in a way that would be appropriate to the original exhibition concept of Karl Ernst Osthaus and Ernst Gosebruch, embracing old and new art, European and non-European art (a form of presentation that was maintained until at least 1937) and that does justice to both the current state of academic research and the new post-colonial world. A start was made by re-arranging the collection in 2005, but there is still much to do in future here, in order to restore the Folkwang Museum's unique identity, true to its founder's intentions, in the German museum landscape.

Hubertus Gassner
DIRECTOR, FOLKWANG MUSEUM

Learning by Seeing

Most neoclassicists took Italy as the starting-point for their art. In Philipp Hackert's case, an essentially realistic streak dominates the otherwise trans-figured landscapes. The **Cave of St. Francis** (Die Franziskushöhle) was a popular tourist destination of the day. Hackert was so taken by the grottoes and caves that he mentions in his letters more than once the fact that he had drawn and painted them. He expressly emphasises the unique and extra-ordinary beauty of nature and the play of the light. They inspired him to produce numerous studies such as the works shown here. Hackert retains the topography of the place, but does not resort to arid replication. Instead he enhances the situation in a painterly, poetic way in the varied play of light and vivid colouring. Even though the drawing can be considered as a sketch for the painting, it retains its inde-pendent pictorial character not least

because of its size and execution in sepia. The only change to introduce a variation into the painting involves the figures. The couple coming out of the

PHILIPP HACKERT
∗ 1737 Prenzlau † 1807 San Piero di Careggio
Cave of St. Francis, 1800
Sepia, brush and pen, 93 × 63 cm
Acquired 1969

GIORGIO SOMMER
∗ 1834 Frankfurt † 1914 Naples
Casa di Melagro, Pompei, c. 1873
Albumen print, 19.6 × 24.5 cm
Acquired 1982

ave with the dog leaping ahead of hem replace the monk going into the ave. Paintings of this kind were soon o be taken over by the still young art of photography, which now captured picturesque places like this on plates, and put a lot of artists out of work. *Fro*

PHILIPP HACKERT
Cave of St. Francis, 1801
Oil on canvas, 126 × 96.5 cm
Acquired 1939

By the late 18th century, the Grand Tour to Italy was obligatory for the educated bourgeoisie and the nobility.
The language was learned as part of the preparation, and visitors made a close study of Italian culture from antiquity onwards. In the 19th century, high-quality ancient ceramics from the Greek motherland were being found in Etruscan tombs, and these artefacts

FRANZ LUDWIG CATEL
∗ 1778 Berlin † 1856 Rome
View from Virgil's Tomb over the City of Naples with the Castel Sant'Elmo, 1818
Oil on canvas, 67.5 × 50 cm
Acquired 2004

became popular collectors' pieces for lovers of Italy. Karl Ernst Osthaus inherited this tradition, and the Folkwang Museum still follows his collecting policy today. This can be seen from

the **amphora** decorated with heavily armed warriors as pictorial decoration and the great **eye bowl** with a depiction of a symposium under vines, one of four known pieces of this kind.

It was customary in the 19th century for artists to accompany travelling friends to see the sights. Thus Franz Ludwig Catel, a central figure among the Germans in Rome, accompanied Prince Galitzin on his journey to Sicily in 1818. They visited **Virgil's Tomb** (Grab des Vergil) in Naples on the way, where Catel painted the prince examining the memorial tablet to the great poet. We look from the shady foreground through a funnel-shaped rock formation whose upper part is overgrown with trees, down to a sunlit district of Naples at a lower level. Beyond this is the hill with the fortress, rising in transparent, atmospheric shade. *Fro*

GREECE, ATTIC

arge eye bowl, Andokides group
. 520 BC
ainted clay, 14.8 cm, Ø at top: 35.6 cm,
ase: 13.9 cm
cquired 1975

GREECE, ATTIC

Neck amphora, c. 520 BC,
Antimenes painter
Painted clay , Ø at top: 17.5 cm, base 13.7 cm
Acquired 1973

Rome was not a large city in the early 19th century. There were numerous vineyards within the Aurelian Walls, and cattle still grazed in the Forum Romanum. But the city of which Goethe said 'there is only one Rome in the world' was a spiritual centre for German artists in particular.

COMTE FRÉDÉRIC FLACHÉRON
✶ 1813 Lyons † post-1883 Paris?
Tempel of Vesta, 1850
Salted paper, 25.1 × 33.1 cm
Acquired 1961

JOSEPH ANTON KOCH
✶ 1768 Tyrol † 1839 Rome
Santa Maria Maggiore in Rome, c. 1808
Oil on canvas, 76.3 × 103 cm
Acquired 1925

Enthusiasm for Rome knew no bounds. Its admirers tried to capture every prospect in pictures. This is how the **Park of the Villa Pamphili** came into being. The picture was commissioned by Crown Prince Maximilian of Bavaria from Johann Christian Reinhart, who actually preferred to paint more imaginative subjects for his topographical works. And yet this piece is a masterpiece in the warmth of its colour. Joseph Anton Koch on the other hand 'improves' the view of the early Christian church of **Santa Maria Maggiore** by populating the Baroque garden of the former Villa Negroni with gardeners and two lovers in old German costume and placing the massive church building tower behind it as a finishing touch. One of the favourite subjects of pictures was the **Temple of Vesta** in Tivoli, a popular day-trip destination not far from Rome. The ruin stands gracefully on an eminence, suggesting poetic transfiguration even in the photograph.

Fro

JOHANN CHRISTIAN REINHART
∗1761 Hof †1847 Rome
Park of the Villa Pamphili, 1832
Oil on canvas, 71 × 101 cm
Acquired 1925

Rottmann painted numerous Italian subjects for King Ludwig I, some of which were later used as models for the fresco decoration in the Munich court arcades. The **Coliseum** (Das Colosseum in Rom) is one of the first pictures the artist painted in Munich after his visit to Italy in 1826/27. It is based on a study he made on the spot, whose composition is substantially the same as that of the painting. The view from the Farnese Gardens shows the ruins of the Coliseum at night, lit by the moon, which is above the amphitheatre. Seeing this ancient building at night was part of the programme for all 19th century visitors to Italy, and is evidence of the romanticising inclinations of our picture as well. Thus for example Eichendorff's *Taugenichts* (Good-for-nothing) character experiences Rome almost exclusively by moonlight. Rottmann emphasises the special nature of this popular subject in his painting by remarking that 'the object is so utterly wonderful … Though the same as has already been treated countless times, it is certainly not seen so often in the celebration of its significance.' Topographical elements that Rottmann sees in Romantic transfiguration are portrayed in modern artists' views of

CARL ROTTMANN
* 1797 Handschuhsheim near Heidelberg
† 1850 Munich

The Coliseum in Rome, 1828
Oil on canvas, 75 × 104.5 cm
Acquired 1942

other cities in all their brutal ugliness. The urban dreariness of **Kreuzberg, Berlin** is underlined by the empty spaces of desolate alleys and streets that seem more hostile than inviting. And the **Fire in Uster** (Brand von Uster), though stagey, also depicts a disastrous situation that addresses the whole questionable nature of modern urban life, in direct contrast to a romanticising view. *Fro*

MICHAEL SCHMIDT
1945 Berlin

Kreuzberg, Berlin, 1981
(from the *Urban Landscapes* series)
Gelatine silver, 13.9 × 28.5 cm
Acquired 2000

PETER FISCHLI ＊1952 Zurich
DAVID WEISS ＊1946 Zurich

Fire in Uster, 1980
C-Print, 50 × 70.2 cm
Acquired 1979

The figures in Joseph Anton Koch's
Landscape with Hercules (Landschaft
mit Herkules am Scheideweg) are not
decorative but staffage intended to add
to the atmosphere of the picture. The
people are integrated into the landscape
as mythological figures, timeless and
idealised. The sun breaks through the
flickering, cloud-covered sky with
dramatic lighting effects, illuminating
the landscape picturesquely and
suddenly picking out the group in the
foreground. The vivid iridescence of
the light and dark tones in combination
with a wash of intermediate hues exudes
aesthetic charm. The exaggerated forms

JOSEPH ANTON KOCH
∗ 1768 Tyrol † 1839 Rome
**Landscape with Hercules
at the Crossroads, c. 1812**
Pen and brush in brown and grey,
with white highlights, 27.5 × 41.7 cm
Acquired pre-1929

HUGO HENNEBERG
∗ 1863 Vienna † 1918 Vienna
Italian Villa in Autumn, 1897
Gum print, 56 × 74.1 cm
Acquired 1979

in this sublime-looking landscape underline the seriousness and dignity of the subject.

Arnold Böcklin replaces the heroic mood of the Hercules image with drama, as the title of the picture suggests. The castle by the sea, a motif that Böcklin used in many pictures, accords with the **Murder in the Castle** (*Mord im Schloss*) ballad by Uhland in its gloomy atmosphere. The contrast between light and dark is particularly important in intensifying the impression of nature. Böcklin admits himself that he struggled to establish the correct proportion for the figures so that interest in them should not outweigh interest in the landscape. The effect of dramatic atmosphere was very much in the air in the second half of the 19th century. Even the photography of the day, like for example Hugo Henneberg's Italian Villa, reflects the picturesque approach. *Fro*

ARNOLD BÖCKLIN
✳ 1827 Basle † 1901 San Domenico
Murder in the Castle, 1859
Oil on canvas, 112 × 177.3 cm
Acquired 1966

In **Bacchus's Feast** (La Fête de Bacchus), figures, some naked and some dressed in ancient garments, are paying homage to the god Bacchus, dancing and playing the harp, with a temple in the background. Corot uses these staffage figures to enhance the impression of an idyll in the atmospheric evening landscape. One special feature is the picturesque harmony of grey-green and silvery shades in the slightly misty atmosphere of the evening. Despite the size of this picture, it has the character of a *paysage intime* in the tradition of the Barbizon School. Böcklin too, following the taste of his times, turns to themes with an ancient cast in numerous paintings, as here in the portrayal of the nature god

JEAN BAPTISTE CAMILLE COROT
✳ 1796 Paris † 1875 Paris

Bacchus's Feast, Evening, 1866
Oil on canvas, 134.5 × 110.5 cm
Acquired 1979

Pan (Pan im Kinderreigen), though he is playing a flute rather than his Pan pipes. The children's round dance contributes to the bucolic cheerfulness of the unfinished painting.

Rodin's sculpture **Faun and Nymph** exudes a markedly sensual charm. The faun is seizing the nymph in an impetuous gesture of rape. Another common title for this group—*Jupiter tauros*—refers to the myth in which Jupiter changed himself into a bull so that he could become intimate with Europa. It is the aesthetic charm of the finely worked block of marble that creates the erotic aura, while the drama of this love struggle is portrayed in a wealth of moving forms, intertwined with complex suppleness. *Kö*

ARNOLD BÖCKLIN
⁎ 1827 Basle † 1901 San Domenico
Pan in the Children's Round Dance, 1884
Mixed technique on mahogany,
79 × 100.1 cm
Acquired by Karl Ernst Osthaus c. 1904

AUGUSTE RODIN
⁎ 1840 Paris † 1917 Paris
Faun and Nymph, 1885/86
Marble, 57.5 cm
Acquired by Karl Ernst Osthaus c. 1903

The **Landscape with Rainbow** (Landschaft mit Regenbogen) emanates a magical, almost unreal atmosphere. The contradictions between the moonlight and the rainbow, between the lighting and the light source, can be explained only in terms of a subjective experience of nature. Tiny humanity is set against the might of nature. The profound darkness, the way the wanderer is looking into the chasm whose depth he cannot divine and the flickering, cloudy sky have something threatening about them. Man is exposed to nature. The rainbow is an ancient symbol for the reconciliation of man with God. Even though man is intended to be part of nature, he is estranged from it. The marked emphasis of the wanderer by lighting effects and his function in the picture as an observer deliberately place him outside nature.

The towering mass of the rocks in the **Uttenwald Gorge** (Uttenwalder Grund), a sight in the Sächsische Schweiz near Dresden, also has a threatening effect.

CASPAR DAVID FRIEDRICH
* 1774 Greifswald † 1840 Dresden
Landscape with Rainbow, 1809/10
Oil on canvas, 70 × 103 cm
Acquired 1948

CASPAR DAVID FRIEDRICH
Uttenwald Gorge, c. 1800
Sepia over pencil, 70.6 × 50 cm
Acquired 1936

In Friedrich's portrayal it contrasts with the light background, the intricate dabs of foliage and the tiny people. The figures' gestures could be interpreted as astonishment and joy at their release from the threatening confines of the gorge. Some people interpret the foreground as the confinement of human existence, the gateway as a symbol of death and the light background as a promise of paradise. This sepia drawing is not a preliminary study for a painting but an independent picture. In his day, Friedrich caused a considerable stir with sepia drawings of this kind. The drawing is incomplete, which explains why it is not possible to make out any variety in tonal values in this sheet. *Fro*

The window looks out on to Saxon elector Augustus the Strong's 'Indian' summer residence at **Schloss Pillnitz**. Dahl portrays what he has seen with all the precision of a *veduta*, including the window reveals and the additional landscape reflected in the panes. The atmospheric, almost poetic treatment of light results from a close friendship with Caspar David Friedrich. The view from the window—effectively a picture within a picture, and in this case pure invention by the artist, whose studio

JOHAN CHRISTIAN DAHL
* 1788 Bergen † 1857 Dresden
View of Schloss Pillnitz, 1823
Oil on canvas, 70 × 45.5 cm
Acquired 1939

GEORG FRIEDRICH KERSTING
* 1785 Güstrow † 1847 Meissen
Woman Knitting at Window, c. 1811
Pencil, pen, Indian ink with wash,
23.1 × 18.7 cm
Acquired 1936

was nowhere near Pillnitz—was a popular 19th century motif. Representing the viewer, the orant figure of a silhouetted **Woman in the Morning Sun** (Frau in der Morgensonne) faces the light of the rising sun. Friedrich's subtle colours illustrate the religious mood of a person confronted with nature. The path, which breaks off so abruptly, may be a metaphor for the end of the path of life. Kersting, a friend of Friedrich, portrays a domestic scene of a **Woman Knitting** (Strickende Frau am Fenster) in affectionate detail, and also takes up the window motif. The young woman has paused briefly in her knitting— her eye and her thoughts are directed somewhere outside the intimate interior at something that remains undefined for us. The silence, time, which seems to stand still, the longing to be at one with nature are also to be found in the film still of a **Needle Woman** from Kimsooja's video— playing with Romantic sensations and motifs in contemporary alienation. *Kö*

KIMSOOJA
* 1957 Taegu
Needle Woman, 1999
Kitakyushu
Video
Acquired 2005

CASPAR DAVID FRIEDRICH
* 1774 Greifswald † 1840 Dresden
Woman in the Morning Sun, c. 1818
Oil on canvas, 22 × 30.5 cm
Acquired 1937

'Two souls dwell, alas, in my breast, and one would like to part from the other,' says doctor and philosopher, lawyer and theologian Faust to his companion Wagner in Scene II of Goethe's tragedy *Faust*, Part I. Carl Gustav Carus shows Faust and Wagner on their **Easter Walk** (Osterspaziergang) outside the city gates in old German Protestant dress as worn at the time by democratic, nationalist-minded progressives, which was banned in 1821. They are both looking at the black poodle, which will later turn out to be Mephistopheles. Carus, like Goethe and the Faust character in his play, was also a learned man. But as a doctor and a

CARL GUSTAV CARUS
* 1789 Leipzig † 1869 Dresden
Easter Walk, 1821
Oil on canvas, 49 × 40 cm
Acquired 1939

scientist, painter and writer, he was entirely able to reconcile the two souls in his breast, one of which concentrates on immediate detail while the other strives for higher knowledge. The contemplative atmosphere of the **View of a Gothic Cathedral** (Blick auf einen Gotischen Dom), in which close-up and distant view are brought together by the window motif, expresses this calm attitude, and so does **Morning Bells** (Frühläuten), with the birds flying peacefully across the sky and the river winding through the plain in the background, which could all quite confidently be read as an allegory on the course of life. In this way the Romantic Carus—he was strongly influenced by Caspar David Friedrich from 1817 to 1827—contributed to the peaceful Biedermeier style. *KyZ*

CARL GUSTAV CARUS
View of a Gothic Cathedral, 1852
Paper, 23.3 × 24.1 cm
Acquired 1922

CARL GUSTAV CARUS
Morning Bells, c. 1840
An old German city in the morning light
Oil on canvas, 100.8 × 71.5 cm
Acquired 1939

Carl Gustav Carus was of a more scientific cast of mind than Caspar David Friedrich. His main occupation was as a medical man, and he was a self-taught artist. He never denied that he was a Romantic—he was a close friend of Friedrich. On his way back from Geneva in 1821 he visited Chamonix, where he took the opportunity of climbing the Montauvert, from which he had a unique view of the Mont Blanc group. Overwhelmed by the sight, which he captured in this painting in 1824, he writes: 'O God, here now is the ideal of the Alpine world I carried within me, really and truly before me.' Apart from his geological interest in the rock formations, the image of the **High Mountains** (Hochgebirge) is Romantically heightened and full of symbolism. The exaggerated height of the Mont Blanc massif with the eternal snow stands for the perpetual divinity, alongside which man becomes visibly insignificant in the form of the three scarcely perceptible walkers on the left by the spruce fir. The dead spruce in the middle points precisely at the peaks of

Mont Blanc, as a sign that life leads to God via death. Despite its sublimity and inapproachability, man tried to conquer wild nature. Many first ascents of the Alpine peaks date from the 19th century. Something that in Carus's day no one dared to do in awe of the divinity and absorbed through contemplation alone, was then attempted in elaborate expeditions, even though these failed all too often, as in the **Abandoned Attempt**. *Fro*

BISSON FRÈRES
AUGUSTE-ROSALIE BISSON
∗ 1826 Paris † 1900 Paris
LOUIS-AUGUSTE BISSON
∗ 1814 Paris † 1876 Paris
Confluence of the Bossons and Taconnal Glaciers (Abandoned Attempt at an Ascent of Mont Blanc), 1859
Albumen print, 23.3 × 38.3 cm
Acquired 1961

CARL GUSTAV CARUS
∗ 1789 Leipzig † 1869 Dresden
High Mountains, c. 1824
Oil on canvas, 136 × 117 cm
Acquired 1938

As a painter, Schinkel counts as a Romantic. Even though the **Landscape near Pichelswerder** (Landschaft bei Pichelswerder) goes back to the contemplation of real nature, the approach is profoundly Romantic. The viewer is looking down at a sweep of countryside that disappears into infinity. The view in the foreground is cut off by a row of dark spruce, but the two figures in the foreground can look over it. Figures with their backs to the viewer and infinite landscapes are formal elements reminiscent of Caspar David Friedrich (cf. p. 44f.).

Morgenstern's **Rocky Landscape** (Felsenlandschaft mit Wildbach) on the other hand represents a younger generation's sense of nature, concentrating on precise, sharp observation. This does not mean superficial realism, however, even though the local features seem to have been captured precisely.

The artist was more interested in an individual statement than a timeless one.

The two drawings by Ludwig Richter, of a **Campagna Landscape** and **Traunfall,** show the same characteristics. In his love of nature, he is more concerned with capturing reality and less with the profound symbolic values of the landscape elements, even though Morgenstern certainly also intended to include the element of fear, of nature going beyond all human scale, that lies behind the visible reality. He found untouched, untamed nature that he could tackle directly in Scandinavia, territory that attracted few travellers at that time. Morgenstern stands for the insight that a rigorous study of reality has to come before sensations of nature, and that acknowledging reality is the painter's real task. *Fro*

KARL FRIEDRICH SCHINKEL
* 1781 Neuruppin † 1841 Berlin
Landscape near Pichelswerder, 1814
Oil on canvas, 62.3 × 96.2 cm
Acquired 1941

ADRIAN LUDWIG RICHTER
∗ 1803 Dresden
† 1884 Loschwitz
Campagna Landscape with Aqueduct, 1825
Pencil, 16.9 × 27.3 cm
Acquired 1906

ADRIAN LUDWIG RICHTER
Traunfall, 1823
Pencil, 19.2 × 24.2 cm
Acquired 1907
Kunstmuseum, Essen

CHRISTIAN ERNST
BERNHARD MORGENSTERN
1805 Hamburg † 1867 Munich
Rocky Landscape with Mountain Torrent, 1828
Oil on canvas, 128 × 100 cm
Acquired 1984

Folkwang Museum, Hagen
Painting gallery looking east, c. 1912

'I am setting up a museum which aims to create an interest in modern art in our art-forsaken industrial area on the Ruhr. As the sole owner of my institution, I am in the happy position of not having to take any prejudices into account and therefore wish to create an attractive building based entirely on modern require- ments and—as far as my means will permit—an exemplary one.'

Karl Ernst Osthaus in a letter
to Henry van de Velde on 26th April 1900

Nulla dies sine linea — no day without a line, was one of Menzel's maxims. He carried a sketchbook with him wherever he went, and captured the life and bustle around him meticulously, 'thinking it through,' as he put it. Throughout his life, reality stimulated him to express the trivial or the inconspicuous, like the lacquer tray that is painted so carefully in the gouache **Travel Plans** (Reisepläne), the teaspoon that has slipped off the saucer and the gleaming beer glass beside it, or the little dog's muzzle dangling from the chair-back. The eye is constantly dispatched on a journey of discovery. The same is true of the pastel **Political Meeting** (Politische Versammlung). A whole variety of attitudes is revealed in the spontaneously drawn faces and the physical poses — lack of interest, fatigue, lively argument, attentiveness and scepticism. But the brilliant draughtsmanship should not let us forget that Menzel was a painter, who could use sophisticated tonal values

ADOLPH VON MENZEL
☀ 1815 Breslau/Wroclaw † 1905 Berlin
Travel Plans, 1875
Gouache on paper, 15.2 × 30.5 cm
Acquired 1938

ADOLPH VON MENZEL
Stairwell with Night Light, 1848
Paper on card, 36 × 21.5 cm
Acquired 1939

and different light-modelling to transform an essentially nondescript corner of a **Stairwell** (Treppenflur bei Nachtbeleuchtung) into an object of artistic enjoyment.

Menzel's new interest in scenes of the world of work as industry burgeoned in the 19th century, which was to culminate in the great painting *The Iron Mill* (Das Eisenwalzwerk, 1875), can be seen a full 20 years earlier in this little **Head Study** (Studienkopf) of a worker with a blue peaked cap. The dignity and self-esteem that shine from these features identify Menzel as a visual person with great insights into human nature. *Kö*

ADOLPH VON MENZEL
Head Study, 1855
Head of a bearded worker with peaked cap
Oil on paper mounted on wood, 35 × 27 cm
Acquired 2000

ADOLPH VON MENZEL
Political Meeting, 1849
Primary electors
Pastel on brown paper, 23.5 × 31.2 cm
Acquired 1940

Evidence of the protracted but constructive dialogue between the realities of painting and photography can be found in the sea pieces by the French painter Gustave Courbet and painter-photographer Le Gray. The study of nature and an eye for the motifs of his home region helped Courbet to find a form as early as the **Oraguay Bluff** (La Roche Oraguay) that portrays the exciting interplay of natural forms and breaks with 19th century tradition.

Le Gray's **Seascape** pictures had caused a stir in the world of landscape photography a few years earlier. His aesthetic claims reside in his painting-like compositions, in the rhythmic integration of wave, cloud and rock formations, and drama created by contrasts between light and shade. Le Gray achieved this atmospheric closeness to reality by copying in a negative, a form of photo-montage. Their related aesthetic ideals and views of nature

GUSTAVE COURBET
* 1819 Ornans † 1877 La-Tour-de-Peilz
Oraguay Bluff, 1860
Vallon de Maisières, Doubs — La Barque
Oil on canvas, 151.5 × 195 cm
Acquired 1968

provide a key to the closeness in terms of image and subject matter found in the landscape impressions of both Courbet and Le Gray. *PS*

JEAN-BAPTISTE GUSTAVE LE GRAY
☀ 1820 Villiers-le-Bel † 1882 Cairo

Seascape, Large Wave, 1856
Albumen print, 34.3 × 41.1 cm
Acquired 1961

GUSTAVE COURBET

Seascape, The Wave, 1870
Marine—La Vague
Oil on canvas, 45 × 59 cm
Acquired 1989

Osthaus established himself as a collector when he purchased Lise (Lise à l'Ombrelle) from Berlin art dealer Paul Cassirer. 'Who is the buyer? And where is Hagen?' was apparently the question Max Liebermann put to Cassirer. Liebermann was not the only person who would like to have acquired the painting—in his case for his private collection. The then director of the National Gallery, Hugo von Tschudi, also wanted it for his institution. Dated 1867, this extraordinary work is closer to mainstream realism or *plein air* painting than to Impressionism, which was just starting to develop. Lise Tréhot, the artist's model, is standing gracefully in bright sunshine in a clearing in the forest of Fontainebleau near Paris. Her face is turned to one side, and shaded by a black lace parasol. The confidence with which he combines a landscape impression with a studio portrait scene is the special feature of this first master-piece by the young Renoir. In the dark-ness of the wood, light is reflected from the damp bark and the leaves of the trees. The high quality of the painting is not revealed only in the white fabric of her dress. Heinrich Kühn photographed **Miss Mary**, who is wearing an equally elaborately tailored lace dress, in a model's typical back view pose. Kühn worked with a calculated distribution of light and shade, and with the blurred focus achieves a painterly effect in the style of pictorialism. Louis Tuaillon also goes back to a classical model pose used since antiquity to depict the **Woman Fastening Her Sandal** (Sandalenbinde-rin). *vL*

HEINRICH KÜHN
∗ 1866 Dresden † 1944 Birgitz
Miss Mary, c. 1906
Oil transfer, 28.6 × 22.2 cm
Acquired 1960

LOUIS TUAILLON
∗ 1862 Berlin † 1919 Berlin
Woman Fastening Sandal, c. 1900
Bronze, 56 cm
Acquired by Karl Ernst Osthaus pre-1912

PIERRE AUGUSTE RENOIR
* 1841 Limoges † 1919 Cagnes
Lise with the Parasol, 1867
Lise à l'ombrelle
Oil on canvas, 184 × 115.5 cm
Acquired by Karl Ernst Osthaus c. 1901

The invention of photography around 1830 meant robust competition for classic portrait painting. Of course painting cannot convey the directness of a photographed subject, as the two differently focused **portrait photographs** by Julia Cameron and Hill and Adamson show. And yet portraits by Wilhelm Leibl and Wilhelm Trübner manage to sustain a high artistic standard. In the **Portrait of Mrs H.** (Bildnis der Frau Regierungsrat H.) Leibl followed the French 1860s style of portrait painting, in 1870 even receiving the Paris Salon's award for the genre. Once back in

JULIA MARGARET CAMERON
* 1815 Calcutta † 1879 Kalutara/Ceylon
Sir John Frederick William Herschel, Baronet, Collingwood/Kent, 1867
Albumen print, 36.1 × 28.1 cm
Acquired 1961

WILHELM LEIBL
* 1844 Cologne † 1900 Würzburg
Portrait of Mrs H., a Senior Official's Wife, 1873
Oil on canvas, 139.5 × 92 cm
Acquired 1998

Germany, Leibl remained in the Chiemgau, where he became the centre of a group that also included Trübner and Sperl. Like the photograph of Hill and Adamson, the two painters emphasize the women's faces and hands. Leibl leaves the clothing and their surroundings in the dark, following the portrait style of the day, while Trübner magnificently renders the heavy fabric the **Lady in Grey** (Dame in Grau) is wearing. Osthaus acquired this and another portrait of a lady by Trübner in 1906, thus bringing the artist new fame. *vL*

DAVID OCTAVIUS HILL
* 1802 Perth † 1870 Newington
ROBERT ADAMSON
* 1821 Burnside † 1848 St. Andrews
**Sir David Brewster, Physicist, Calotypist,
Principal of United College St. Andrews,
Vice-Chancellor of Edinburgh University, c. 1844**
Calotype, 19.8 × 14.4 cm, acquired 1979

WILHELM TRÜBNER
* 1851 Heidelberg † 1917 Karlsruhe
Lady in Grey, 1877
Oil on canvas, 92.8 × 78 cm
Acquired by Karl Ernst Osthaus c. 1906

One of the most unusual pictures in the collection in its formal structure and colouring is Daumier's **Ecce Homo**, with the anonymous mass surging around the execution block, the bold foreshortening of the demagogue figure and the accused, who is emphasised by colouring reminiscent of artists such as Goya or Rembrandt, highlighting the isolation of anyone who dares oppose popular opinion. This is a subject that in the 19th century in particular touches on the problems of the artist's position in society, and the picture is probably to be interpreted in this rather than the Christian sense.

In his **Faure as Hamlet** (Portrait de Chanteur Faure) Manet creates a sense of theatricality by his brilliant reproduction of light: Hamlet, whose eyes, wide with terror, speak of his meeting with his murdered father and has just drawn his sword. This picture not only identifies Manet as a master of Impressionism but is also one of the 19th century's few great theatrical portrayals. Rodin uses the body of a naked youth to express an abstract idea: a human being become aware of growing up through a subconscious presentiment—dead matter given life by the artist's shaping hand to become a statement. **The Bronze Age** (L'Âge

EDOUARD MANET
✳ 1832 Paris † 1883 Paris
Singer Jean Baptiste Faure as Hamlet, 1877
Portrait de Chanteur Faure dans le Rôle
d'Hamlet
Oil on canvas, 194 × 131.5 cm
Acquired 1927

AUGUSTE RODIN
✳ 1840 Paris † 1917 Meudon
The Bronze Age, c. 1880
L' Âge d'Airin
Bronze, 180.5 cm
Acquired by Karl Ernst Osthaus c. 1901

d'Airain) is when the time we move
out of the blissful fields of paradise to
be confronted with the real world.
This too is a form of show — showing
an idea, though a rather subtler, less
theatrical one. *Kö*

HONORÉ DAUMIER
· 1808 Marseille † 1879 Valmondois

Ecce Homo, c. 1851
Oil on canvas, 162.3 × 130.5 cm
Acquired by Karl Ernst Osthaus in 1906

The gestures and attitudes of these three women could not be more different: the expression of profound shame after being driven out of paradise, the self-confident pose of the woman in the kitchen and the quirky portrait. In her self-portrait in the form of an **untitled film still**, Cindy Sherman successfully stages a scene that subverts the heteronormative view of women. She uses the classic cliché in a particularly challenging way to this end, while Gertrud Arndt at the Bauhaus explores photography and its experimental possibilities, for example in the **mask portrait** (Maskenbildnis) double exposure of her youthfully naïve and fresh face.

Rodin originally his intended **Eve** as one of the large figures for the representation of the gates of Hell that he had been working on for the French state since 1880. She and Adam were to flank a gigantic portal. That idea was never carried out, but the Eve was executed as an individual figure in various materials. 'The crucial factor in this choice,' said Osthaus on acquiring the sculpture, 'was Rodin's explanation that this was the birth of Impressionism in his work.' *vL*

AUGUSTE RODIN
∗ 1840 Paris † 1917 Meudon
Eve, c. 1881
Bronze, 174 cm
Acquired by Karl Ernst Osthaus c. 1901

ERTRUD ARNDT
1903 Ratibor † 2000 Darmstadt

ask Portrait no. 16, Dessau, 1930
elatine silver bromide, 21.8 × 16.4 cm
cquired 1984

CINDY SHERMAN
∗ 1954 Glen Ridge

Untitled filmstill, 1977
Gelatine silver, 16 × 23.1 cm
Acquired 1985

Max Liebermann came closer to Impressionism that almost any other German artist. No picture illustrates this better than **The Parrot Man** (Der Papageienmann). Even though the artist's observations in Amsterdam Zoo were not processed until he was back in the studio, it looks as though it was painted directly from a live model. Liebermann uses a spontaneous speed technique to concentrate on conveying a first impression in glowing colours. Following his maxim 'drawing is omission', his colour are deployed to reveal essentials only. Despite the bright colours and his preference for translucent leaf canopies that capture that brightness and lightness of a summer's day, the achievements of naturalism are not abandoned Liebermann remains a sharp observer, despite skimping on the details of objects. He retains a spatial order

LOVIS CORINTH
* 1858 Tapiau † 1925 Zandvoort
Thomas in Armour, 1909
Oil on canvas, 45.8 × 55.8 cm
Acquired 1942

MAX LIEBERMANN
* 1847 Berlin † 1935 Berlin
The Parrot Man, 1902
Oil on canvas, 102.5 × 72.5 cm
Acquired 1914

that opens up to us in chronological sequence.

Corinth's late work represents an opposite view. At the end of his life, the subject increasingly became an image of his inner self. This also applies to his portrait of his son Thomas in Armour, painted in the year of his death. The skin of the picture is torn open, and the violent brushwork destroys anything representational. Corinth offers no modelling, nor investigates the material consistency of surfaces, but makes the figure, whose forms disintegrate before our eyes, into a shadowy presence. For Corinth, capturing reality becomes a metaphor of existential experience. *Fro*

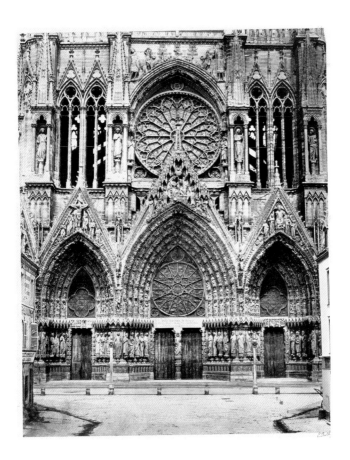

Monet opened up an aspect of serial painting around 1890 with his picture series on a variety of subjects that still look up-to-date and modern. Serial motifs, whether as we know them in Andy Warhol's painting today or in the documentary photography of Bernd and Hilla Becher, turned out to be something that would create a style, and could also be monumental in their three-dimensional effect. In 1892/93, Monet painted about 30 almost identical pictures of the façade of **Rouen Cathedral**, seen from the building opposite the west façade. Different times of day, atmosphere and light, weather and personal mood led Monet to vary the picture constantly. Monet shows the key section of the façade slightly from the left, the three doorways with the rose window above them and the gallery of kings. Only the glow on the tip of the busy façade reliefs enable the viewer to makes sense of the cathedral

EDOUARD-DÉNIS BALDUS
* 1815 Grünebach † 1882 Arcueil-Cachan near Paris

Rheims Cathedral, 1852–1860
Albumen print, 42 × 32.9 cm
Acquired 1961

CLAUDE MONET
* 1840 Paris † 1926 Giverny

Rouen Cathedral in Mist (The Doorway), 189
Le Portail
Oil on canvas, 101 × 66 cm
Acquired 1970

architecture in the misty morning light. The austere and sober view of the west end of **Rheims Cathedral** in the photograph shows the degree of abstraction Monet opts for in the treatment of the richly figured High Gothic façades and their tracery, while bringing out the huge importance of church architecture as it developed from cathedral to cathedral in the 12th and 13th centuries. *vL*

The two paintings by Paul Cézanne that Karl Ernst Osthaus acquired in Paris shortly after the master's death in 1906 are among the collection's outstanding treasures. Osthaus had already visited Cézanne, who was living reclusively in Aix, in April 1902, and returned in 1906 to talk about acquisitions.

Cézanne must have painted the **Maison de Bellevue and Dovecote** (Maison de Bellevue et Pigeonnier) near Aix-en-Provence between 1888 and 1892. He was already much admired in his lifetime by the next generation of artists for his novel style, and here he places his colours with almost no consideration for the actual circumstances, defining a not particularly spectacular view of Mediterranean architecture with great effect. This balanced landscape is airy as a watercolour, delicate, and fragrant with the atmosphere of high summer.

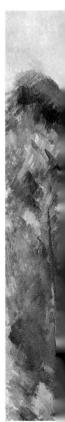

PAUL CÉZANNE
∗ 1839 Aix-en-Provence † 1906 Aix-en-Provence
Maison de Bellevue and Dovecote, c. 1890
Maison de Bellevue et Pigeonnier
Oil on canvas, 65 × 81.2 cm
Acquired by Karl Ernst Osthaus 1907

The **Quarry at Bibémus** (Carrière de Bibémus), also not far from Aix-en-Provence, is probably the first depiction of this abandoned quarry in a broken, rocky massif. Cézanne uses glazing brushstrokes in pastel shades to arrange heavy masses of vertical stone walls with airy lightness, placing areas of shadow in contrast with contrasting colour shades of orange rock and purplish blue sky, with treetops in front forming a horizon with their blurred outlines. After the first raids on pictures in 1937, this was one of the paintings the Nazis confiscated in order to earn foreign currency—it was one of the museum's most severe losses. Happier circumstances meant that the Folkwang was able to acquire the painting for a second time in 1964. *vL*

PAUL CÉZANNE
The Quarry at Bibémus, 1895
La Carrière de Bibémus
Oil on canvas, 63.5 × 79 cm
Acquired by Karl Ernst Osthaus 1906
Confiscated 1937, reacquired 1964

Osthaus acquired several works by Belgian sculptor Constantin Meunier through Henry van de Velde. Meunier was particularly interested in portraying workers, including the tall **Stevedore** (Débardeur). He stands in a confident pose, his hand on his hips, showing the viewer his muscular body, thinly covered with protective working clothes. Unlike Van Gogh's **Peasant Gleaning** (Paysanne Arrachant de l'Herbe), the debilitating work required of day labourers seems to have made little impression on him. The woman is working over the harvested cornfield again, stooping for every ear that is left. This powerful chalk drawing comes from the artist's early first phase in which social subjects like the everyday life of farmers or weavers provided subject matter for his work.

Osthaus also acquired the Pointillist-style picture of a **Steelworks** (L'Aciérie à

MAXIMILIEN LUCE
* 1858 Paris † 1941 Paris

Steelworks, Couillet, 1900
L'Aciérie à Couillet
Oil on canvas, 73.3 × 92.8 cm
Acquired by Karl Ernst Osthaus pre-1905

CONSTANTIN MEUNIER
* 1831 Etterbeek † 1905 Ixelles

Stevedore, 1893
Le Débardeur
Bronze, 213 cm
Acquired 1929

Couillet) by the Belgian artist Maximilian Luce relatively soon after the museum was founded. Osthaus's Hagen museum was still lacking in labour scenes to hang alongside the French Pointillists Seurat, Signac and Cross, whose landscapes and port views had already taken up their places in the museum. This was all the more important as the overwhelming majority of people in the Hagen region worked in the coal, iron and steel-making industries. Perhaps stimulated by Adolf Menzel's *Iron Mill*, famed for its realism, fifty years later Luce showed how the workers of the day were constantly exposed to heat, and how they even had to take their breaks in the

immediate vicinity of their workplace during the long shifts. Tapping the liquid gold or rolling the cooling iron dominated their hard day's work. *vL*

VINCENT VAN GOGH
* 1853 Groot-Zundert † 1890 Auvers-sur-Oise
Peasant Gleaning, 1885
Paysanne Arrachant de l'Herbe
Black chalk, 51.5 × 41.5 cm
Acquired by Karl Ernst Osthaus 1909

The Kelp Harvesters (Les Ramasseuses de Varech) is a magnificent masterpiece with which Gauguin said goodbye to Europe in painterly as well as thematic terms, but not without referring for the last time to the great figures of French Impressionism he so admired—the style of an artist like Paul Cézanne, for example, or the compositional sophistication of someone like Edgar Degas. And not least, the Uccello-esque cropped foreleg of a horse also clearly shows his profound knowledge of Florentine Renaissance painting. Osthaus was Gauguin's first German collector, bringing eight paintings by this highly individual Frenchman together in his museum in Hagen. As well as the depictions of the Breton world of fishermen and peasants, visitors were confronted by what was perhaps the most distinctive work of art in the Folkwang collection as they entered the building, the Fountain with Kneeling Boys by Belgian sculptor George Minne. At the request of Henry van de Velde, Minne produced a variant of the cool and seemingly eccentric fountain first shown in the Vienna Secession in 1906/06. The fountain with its five absolutely identical boys in white marble looking into the basin was set

GEORGE MINNE
Fountain with Kneeling Boys, 1900/1905–06
Marble, 169 cm
Acquired by Karl Ernst Osthaus c. 1905

up in the entrance hall in 1905/06.
The museum already had a selection of
the sculptor's work on show in 1903,
including the **Man with Wineskin**
(L'Homme à l'Outre). The striking
feature of Minne's sculptures is the
sometimes distorted and exaggerated
pose of the body and limbs, which—
as is evident from Hodler's *Spring*
(p. 97)—probably made a lasting
impression on Viennese artists such
as Schiele or Kokoschka. Although it is
designed quite differently in formal
terms, the elegiac pose of the Breton
seaweed harvester in the foreground
of Gauguin's picture is comparable
with the unselfconscious pose of
Minne's boy. It reflects a widespread,
essentially *fin de siècle* attitude. *vL*

PAUL GAUGUIN
* 1848 Paris † 1903 Atuana
The Kelp Gatherers, 1889
Les Ramasseuses de Varech
Oil on canvas, 87 × 123.1 cm
Acquired by Karl Ernst Osthaus c. 1903

GEORGE MINNE
* 1866 Ghent † 1941 Laethem-St. Martin
Man with Wineskin, 1897
L'Homme à l'Outre
Marble, 66.5 cm
Acquired by Karl Ernst Osthaus pre-1909

In autumn 1905, Osthaus showed eleven pictures by Van Gogh in his museum, which he obtained through Johanna Cohen-Gosschalk-Bonger, the widow of the artist's brother Theo van Gogh. It is to be assumed that the collector made a selection from this group, and later opened up a new and important aspect of contemporary painting in his still young collection with the acquisition of these magnificent paintings by Van Gogh through Paul Cassirer in Berlin. They include the unusually pure portrait, its contrasting colours bringing out the powerful presence, against an almost totally uninformative background, of sixteen-year-old **Armand Roulin**, whom Van Gogh shows as very grown-up in 1888. This impression is certainly underlined by the face, no doubt bronzed by the southern sun, and a three-day beard, and the official clothing with a greeny yellow jacket over a dark blue

waistcoat and a broad-brimmed straw hat with a wide band. The young man's father was the postman in Arles. The artist had made friends with him, as is borne out by numerous portraits of him and his family.

It was Ernst Gosebruch who bought the **Moored Boats** (Les Bateaux Amarrés) from Druet in Paris in 1912 for the Essen Kunstmuseum; their

cargo of sand is just being unloaded by workers with wheelbarrows. 'The two boats are purple-pink, the water is a powerful green, no sky, a tricolour on the mast,' was van Gogh's laconic description of the painting to his painter friend Emil Bernard. *vL*

VINCENT VAN GOGH
* 1853 Groot-Zundert † 1890 Auvers-sur-Oise
Armand Roulin, 1888
Portrait of a Young Man
Oil on canvas, 65 × 54.1 cm
Acquired by Karl Ernst Osthaus c. 1903

VINCENT VAN GOGH
Moored Boats, 1888
Les Bateaux Amarrés
Oil on canvas, 55.1 × 66.2 cm
Acquired 1912 by Kunstmuseum, Essen

Vincent van Gogh painted the stone-walled **Hospital Park** (Le Parc de l'Hôpital) of the Saint-Rémy mental hospital the artist had checked into on the advice of Dr. Gachet because of acute mood swings. We know from a letter to Emil Bernard the effect the sight of the park belonging to the psychiatric hospital had on the artist: 'On the right a grey terrace, a bit of the building. A few withered rose-bushes, on the left the park—red ochre—terrain burned by the sun, covered with fallen spruce needles … A wall—also red ochre—blocks out the view and then a little purple and yellow ochre mound rises over it at one point. The first tree is a gigantic trunk, but struck by lightning and sawn off; though one side branch does still stick out, shedding a shower of dark-green needles. This gloomy giant … contrasts with the pale smile of a late rose wilting on the

JAPAN
Ming bowl
[presumably 19C]
Porcelain, lacquer and gold paint,
6.5 cm; Ø 27.5 cm
[Karl Ernst Osthaus Collection]

bush opposite. Under the pines empty stone benches and a dark box tree, the sky is reflected in a puddle—yellow— after a shower of rain. A ray of sunlight, the last reflection, heightens the dark ochre to gleaming orange. Small black figures move around to and fro between the tree-trunks.' The strikingly ornamental arrangement of the trees and treetops is reminiscent of Japanese craftsmanship. European art had acquired a taste for things Japanese from 1870 or earlier, when Japan largely opened its borders to trade. Woodcuts by Hokusai depicting landscapes, theatre scenes or scenes from religious events became just as popular as valuable plates or items like this Ming bowl, lavishly decorated with stylised tree and landscape motifs. *vL*

VINCENT VAN GOGH
☀ 1853 Groot-Zundert † 1890 Auvers-sur-Oise
The Hospital Park, 1889
Le Parc de l'Hôpital
Oil on canvas, 73.1 × 92.6 cm
Acquired by Karl Ernst Osthaus pre-1906

VINCENT VAN GOGH
∗ 1853 Groot-Zundert † 1890 Auvers-sur-Oise
View of the Crau, 1888
Vue de la Crau
Pencil/pen/brush on paper, 30.9 × 47.7 cm
Acquired by Karl Ernst Osthaus in 1909

VINCENT VAN GOGH
The Reaper, 1889
Le Moissonneur
Oil on canvas, 59.5 × 72.5 cm
Acquired by Karl Ernst Osthaus in 1902

On the other side of the stone wall around the garden of Saint-Rémy hospital, the view opens out on to a wide plain with a hilly landscape beyond. Van Gogh was able to observe this every day through his window, and it inspired him to produce the wonderful **The Reaper** (Le Moissoneur) painting of a sulphur-yellow cornfield ripe for harvest. Van Gogh repeated this subject in almost identical pictures or did similar landscapes such as the **View of the Crau** (Vue de la Crau) or *Landscape with Cypresses*. Van Gogh expressed his feelings about this picture in a letter to his brother Theo: 'I see this reaper as an indeterminate figure, struggling like the devil in overpowering heat to get his work done; I see an image of death in him, in the sense that people are the corn that is being sickled down. So it is, if you like, a counterpart to the sower I attempted earlier. But there is nothing sad about this death, it is happening in broad daylight, with the sun flooding everything with light like fine gold.' Like in the wavy, winding decoration on the Japanese bowl, here too in the Japanese *suzuribako* or **writing box** the natural grain of the root wood is taken into account, providing additional decorative charm alongside the reliefs of the tortoises. It was applied art of this kind from Asia that enthused not just Van Gogh and his contemporaries, but also the Nabis artists who followed them. *vL*

JAPAN
Lid of a writing box, 18/19C
Wood, coloured lacquer, 21.1 × 18.9 × 4.1 cm
Acquired by Karl Ernst Osthaus

The **Madonna with Child** (Vierge au Baiser), painted c. 1900 by Denis in these special, pastel tones shows his wife Marthe as a Madonna holding her daughter Anne-Marie, who is only a few months old, up to a window in their Paris flat, with a view of the Le Prieuré hospital behind.

Sculptor Medardo Rosso, who was based in Paris from 1902, was notable not just for his subject matter, portraits of children (e.g. **Child in the Sun**). It was important to him to understand the craft production of sculpture as an artistic process. He was not content to leave everything to the foundry after executing the sculptures in plaster or wax. So he experimented with the casting process, adding substances like sand to the casting material but then doing no further work, thus achieving the un-usual and unmistakable result of

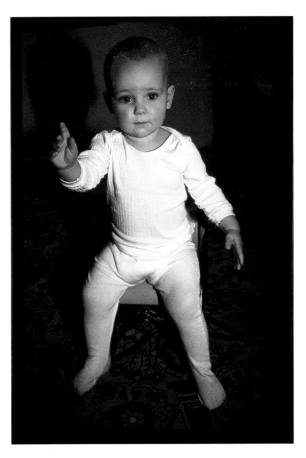

NAN GOLDIN
* 1953 Washington

Ulrika, 1998
Cibachrome, 103 × 119 cm
Acquired 1999

MAURICE DENIS
* 1870 Granville † 1945 Saint-Germain-en-Lay

Madonna with Child (The Kiss), 1902
Vierge au Baiser
Oil on canvas, 99 × 82 cm
Acquired by Karl Ernst Osthaus in 1904

lasting as a process to be accepted and inherent in the work. Nan Goldin's portrait of **Ulrika** also manages to combine various associations—e.g. a religious quality and expressive gentleness. The gesture conveys the simultaneity of their proverbial maturity with the wise eye for the future that many babies seem to have at a certain age. *vL*

MEDARDO ROSSO
1858 Turin † 1928 Milan
Child in the Sun, 1892
Bambino al Sole
Bronze, 38 cm
Acquired by Karl Ernst Osthaus pre-1912

Osthaus acquired Paul Gauguin's **Woman with Fan** (Femme à l'Éventail), painted in Atuona in 1902, from Ambroise Vollard. She was not a princess, as one might assume, but Tohotaua, the wife of his cook. She has a girlish grace, magnificent hair of a brownish-chestnut colour and is wearing a white lavalava, a calico cloth slung round her hips. She has a white feather fan in her right hand and is sitting—somewhat bored and yet majestic—on a chair lavishly decorated with carvings. Gauguin painted the cockade of the white feather fan in the French national colours blue, white and red, a critical comment on the Grande Nation's insensitive approach—France had annexed Tahiti and the Marquesas in 1880—that occurs frequently in his work. Gauguin paints Tohotaua in reflective mood, turned in on herself, indifferent. Paul Graham's **portrait** of a young woman captivating the viewer

PAUL GRAHAM
∗ 1956 Stafford

Page from the *God in Hell* album, 1993
C-Print, paper, 40 × 30 cm
Acquired 1997

with her charming smile seems frank and full of *joie de vivre* in comparison, though she is trying to cover her mouth with her hand with typically Japanese reticence. How much do we Europeans understand when looking at something alien yet familiar, today or a century ago? *vL*

PAUL GAUGUIN
* 1848 Paris † 1903 Atuana

Woman with Fan, 1902
Femme à l'Éventail
Oil on canvas, 91.9 × 72.9 cm
Acquired by Karl Ernst Osthaus in 1904

Gauguin's fascination with Tohotaua's beautiful appearance moved him to immortalise her again in what is perhaps his most beautiful and mysterious painting, the **Barbarian Tales** (Contes Barbares), also dating from 1902. Tohotaua is kneeling in the foreground as the embodiment of animist religions. Behind her is a young man in the pose of a Buddha, personifying Buddhism. The mysterious-looking portrait of his friend Jacob Meyer de Haan stands for the Judaeo-Christian religion.

As early as 1889 Gauguin had painted a portrait of de Haan in *Nirvana* as a being similar to the devil. Thirteen years later Gauguin repeated this diabolical-looking portrait with the pointed chin, gleaming green eyes, flat nose and flaming, fiery-red hair in the middle of a South Sea landscape. Past and present meet in this picture, inspired by the seriously ill artist's longing for death, which can clearly be discerned. Clouds of white smoke give the impression of clouds passing after a refreshing shower of

ANDRES SERRANO
* 1950 New York
The Interpretation of Dreams (Black Santa), 2001
C-Print, 101.6 × 82.6 cm
Acquired 2002

JAPAN
Buddha of the Healing, Yakushi Nyorai, 17/18C
Wood, gold lacquer finish, 52 cm
Acquired 1927

rain, the fruit of paradise is set down like a costly sacrifice, and the lilies are a symbol of the proclamation of life and death at the same time.

While the Yakushi Noyorai Buddha of healing gets steadily closer to a paradisiacal existence in Nirvana with his daily spiritual exercises and much meditation, traditional social boundaries are set for the Black Santa Father Christmas photographed by Serrano, despite the efforts he takes (typical of this photographer) to stage a dark-skinned St. Nicholas. The longing for perfect understanding and a carefree existence is man's most fervent desire, independently of society, skin colour and religion. *vL*

PAUL GAUGUIN
∗ 1848 Paris † 1903 Atuana

Barbarian Tales, 1902
Contes Barbares
Oil on canvas, 131.5 × 90.5 cm
Acquired by Karl Ernst Osthaus c. 1903

Gauguin is presumably addressing vanitas symbolism in the third painting, **Horsemen on the Beach** (Cavaliers sur la Plage) that Osthaus acquired, again from Ambroise Vollard, from the artist's last series of works from Altuona. Two messengers of death come tearing in from the left, their faces masked, their bodies covered with Capuchin cloaks, directly and deliberately crossing the path of three other riders on the beach on their way to the water. The two-dimensional treatment and colours used make the two figures on horseback seem unreal, as though not belonging to the same reality as the three figures with their backs to us. In fact they come from an Indian relief

PAUL GAUGUIN
* 1848 Paris † 1903 Atuana
Riders on the Beach, 1902
Cavaliers sur la Plage
Oil on canvas, 65.6 × 75.9 cm
Acquired by Karl Ernst Osthaus in 1904

that is organised in the same frieze-like and silhouetted way as the riders on the Attic grave vessel. Taming horses and making them into faithful companions in times of peace or war was a skill that mankind had acquired even in ancient times. While Gauguin's horsemen tell of transience, the master of the **kyathos** decorates the outer wall of the vessel with a cavalcade of mounted warriors. The handle of this vessel, obviously intended as a grave good, terminates in a lion's head at the rim. This special feature indicates that the piece originated in Etruria. Only 15 examples of this classical single-handled kyathos are known anywhere. *vL*

GREECE, ATTIC
Large kyathos on high base, 510–500 BC
Single-handled kantharos
Clay, with handle, 27.3 cm, Ø cup: 20.2 cm, base: 11.5 cm
Acquired by Karl Ernst Osthaus

Folkwang Museum, Essen,
following reorganisation in 1929

'Transplanted to the heart of the industrial area, Folkwang would have to become a true fountain of life, an unfailing source of the most abundant blessing, and its collections optimally combine the enjoyment of art with an introduction to and instruction in the history of culture, meeting the purposes of popular education in exemplary fashion.'

Ernst Gosebruch, 1922

Still life does not describe a uniform genre. Its motifs can be of natural or artistic origin, or be arranged elements from the everyday world. The still life became a subject for the avant-garde from the 1860s, as it offered the opportunity for autonomous picture designs.

Belgian artist James Ensor is considered the forerunner of Expressionism. His output was driven by combining the real and the unreal. Thus **Le Chou Frisé** (The Savoy Cabbage) has the savoy cabbage in the centre, with supposedly human features; a lifeless tongue seems to be

IRVING PENN
* 1917 Plainfield
Turducken, 1999
C-Print, 76 × 60.5 cm
Acquired 2002

hanging out of the mouth. The red table is reminiscent of a bloody scaffold, and dramatises the setting. The French term *nature morte* could be translated literally here. Photographer Irving Penn has focused on still lifes as a genre since the beginning of his career. **Turducken** (1999) shows three oven-ready poultry items pushed into each other— a turkey, a duck and a chicken. The lighting emphasises the nakedness of the plucked creatures. They lie on the sterile white dissecting table, vulnerable but also obscene in their 'copulation'. The conventional kitchen still life, photographed with cool precision, flips over into unreality— just as in Ensor. *CK*

JAMES ENSOR
⁎ 1860 Ostend † 1949 Ostend
The Savoy Cabbage, 1894
Le Chou Frisé
Oil on canvas, 80 × 100 cm
Acquired 1961

In spring 1905 Karl Ernst Osthaus showed five works by Ferdinand Hodler at the Folkwang, buying **Spring** (Frühling), the first work by the artist to be sold outside Switzerland. Hodler had shown this work at the Vienna Secession after its first appearance at the Schweizerischer Kunstverein in Zurich in 1901. Then he rethought the subject and showed it in changed form in 1904 as part of a more extensive exhibition of his work in Vienna, gaining considerable fame. At the centre of the painting is the maturing, eccentric-looking Hector, Hodler's son, who is having life, or artistic inspiration, 'blown' into him by

a muse, the artist's niece. Hector's seated pose and the position of his arms are particularly striking—highly mannered and exaggerated. This weird body position, also found in Minne's fountain boys and *Man with Wineskin* (p. 77), was soon to be repeated in the work of Kokoschka and Schiele,

ARISTIDE MAILLOL
✳ 1861 Banyuls-sur-Mer † 1944 Banyuls-sur-M
The Racing Cyclist, 1907/08
Le Coureur Cycliste
Bronze, 98 cm
Acquired by Karl Ernst Osthaus pre-1912

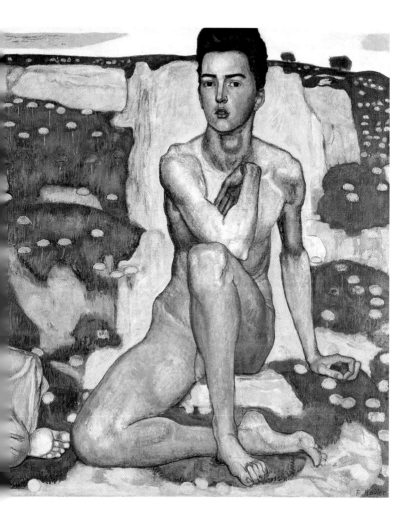

becoming a definitive feature of their style. The young Aristide Maillol shaped **The Racing Cyclist** (Le Coureur Cycliste) in comparable, if not quite so extravagant fashion. This bronze with its extremely fine surface was cast for Harry, Graf Kessler using the lost-wax technique in 1907/08. Kessler had asked Maillol to immortalize his friend, the young Parisian racing cyclist Gaston Colin, in this half lifesize work, ordering four copies. *vL*

FERDINAND HODLER
∗ 1853 Berne † 1918 Geneva

Spring, 1901
Oil on canvas, 105 × 131 cm
Acquired by Karl Ernst Osthaus in 1905

It is not just their elegant form that makes these **three goblets**, presumably from Cyprus, so attractive, but their decoration as well. This consists of simple, flowing incised drawings, based on ideas from early Iranian ceramics, which ultimately provided models for the famous Italian *sgraffito* ware of the 15th century.

Henri Matisse also brought a series of ceramic objects with comparably painterly, patchy decoration and flowing linear ornaments together in his famous **Asphodel** (L'Asphodèle) still life, painted in 1907 and acquired by Karl Ernst Osthaus for the Folkwang in the same year. The surface of the picture is lent articulation and rhythm by the almost draughtsmanlike curves of the bending lily stems, the rounded forms of the pottery and the bizarrely proliferating leaves of the plant in the foreground.

Matisse was one of the leading artists of the Fauve group, whose principal creative resource was pure, powerful colour enhanced by contrasts, arranged decoratively on the surface. It is the suggestive power of colour, combined with the draughtsman's control of the brushstrokes, that give the picture its euphony, in accordance with Matisse's own words: 'A work of art must carry its entire meaning within itself and convey it to the viewers, even before they can identify the subject.' *Kö*

CYPRUS
Three goblets, 14/15C
Earthenware, light slip, brownish-yellow, greenish glazing flecks, incised patterning,
Left: 11 cm, ø 13 cm, centre: 12.5 cm, ø 13 cm, right: 11.5 cm, ø 14 cm
Acquired by Karl Ernst Osthaus

HENRI MATISSE
* 1869 Le Cateau † 1954 Cimiez
Asphodel, 1907 (1906)
L'Asphodèle
Oil on canvas, 116.5 × 89 cm
Acquired by Karl Ernst Osthaus in 1907

We have admired the symmetry of the Egyptian queen **Nefertiti**'s features for thousands of years. This delicate head in the highly refined Amarna style once topped one of the 14 boundary stelae around the Tell el-Amarna temple precinct.

Ancient Egyptian art also inspired 20th century artists. Paula Modersohn-Becker, for example, also modelled her **self-portrait** on an Egyptian mummy, as the lines coming to a conical point in the background and the large, wide-open eyes indicate. A subtle smile plays around her mouth, and in her hand she carries an evergreen twig—she was expecting her first daughter and had no premonition that this would be her last

PAULA MODERSOHN-BECKER
* 1876 Dresden † 1907 Worpswede
Self-Portrait with Camellia Twig, 1906/07
Oil on wood, 61.5 × 30.5 cm
Acquired by Karl Ernst Osthaus in 1913, confiscated in 1937, reacquired 1957

self-portrait. In contrast, Wilhelm Lehmbruck's **Standing Female Figure** (Stehende) comes close to the formal expectations of classical antiquity. A sense of relaxed repose, reflection and also a melancholy dreaminess characterise the sculpture. It is one of the classical female figures that the artist in Paris made as a response to anti-classical work by Auguste Rodin and the neoclassicist Aristide Maillol. *Kö*

EGYPT
Head of Nefertiti from a Tell el-Amarna boundary stele, 1343 BC
Crystal limestone, 31 cm
Acquired 1961

WILHELM LEHMBRUCK
* 1881 Meiderich † 1919 Berlin
Standing Female Figure, 1910
Woman Bathing
Bronze, 194 cm
Acquired 1928

The **Seine at Saint-Cloud** is the first picture by the painter Signac to be acquired by a German museum, being already in the Hagen Folkwang collection by 1905. Signac and his great model Seurat, exponents of Pointillism and Neo-Impressionism, wanted to go beyond the Impressionists' visual perception and enhance the treatment of colour. Signac saw representing atmospheric light as painting's actual role. In order to do this, he chose the colours created when light is refracted in a prism. Placed on the canvas in the

CHRISTIAN ROHLFS
✳ 1849 Niendorf b. Leezen † 1938 Hagen
Birch Wood, 1907
Oil on canvas, 110 × 75 cm
Acquired by Karl Ernst Osthaus pre-1910, confiscated in 1937, reacquired 1958

form of many little dots, the artists left the eye to mix the colours additively and make the shapes. In this way he portrays a summer's day on the Seine. Above the river, it is just possible to sense the presence of Saint-Cloud in the distance, through a misty veil. Seven years later Rohlfs, who had his studio at the Hagen Folkwang, conjured up the intoxication of autumn colours in a sunlit **birch wood** (Birkenwald) with expressive brushstrokes, but with a perception of light that is no less sensitive. The spontaneously placed flecks with their many colour mixtures, placed within and over each other, give the impression of light flickering through autumn woodland foliage. *Kö*

PAUL SIGNAC
* 1863 Paris † 1935 Paris
The Seine at Saint-Cloud, 1899
Saint-Cloud
Oil on canvas, 65 × 81.2 cm
Acquired by Karl Ernst Osthaus in 1905

As a rule, Kirchner's models were his partner or close friends, like here. Doris Grosse, nicknamed Dodo, was a milliner by trade and lived with Kirchner in Dresden from 1908 to 1911. She had a womanly body and luxuriant black hair. Her enormous hats are the subject of numerous paintings and drawings. These works also provide eloquent evidence of the artist's domestic arrangements, the iron, coal-fired stove, for example, with ceramics he

ERNST LUDWIG KIRCHNER
∗ 1880 Aschaffenburg
† 1938 Frauenkirch
Female Nude, c. 1909
Chalk, 44.5 × 34.5 cm
Acquired 1953

HUGO WILHELM BERTHOLD ERFURTH
∗ 1874 Halle † 1948 Gaienhofen
Portrait of a Girl in a Hat, c. 1902
Bromoil print, 30 × 23.7 cm
Acquired in 1979

has made himself on it, or the sleeping tent set up in the studio, also decorated with love scenes by Kirchner, as can be seen at the back of the **drawing**. Kirchner's drawing and **painting** style shows a rapid, restless hand. Powerful colour tones like orange, red and blue are juxtaposed impudently, and the flesh tones of the nude itself are defined very physically, with bright colours. Despite all the generosity in the treatment of detail, the painted portrait of Dodo contrasts in terms of expressiveness and intimate liberality with the somewhat earlier **Portrait of a Girl with Hat** (Mädchenporträt mit Hut) by Hugo Erfurth, probably an official portrait. Erfurth photographs a young woman against an extensive, slightly hilly landscape. She is wearing a lavish hat decorated with real flowers over her hair, which is pinned up, perhaps for some auspicious occasion like going to church or a wedding. Neckband and traditional costume suggest an origin in southern Baden. *vL*

ERNST LUDWIG KIRCHNER
Seated Nude on Orange Cloth, 1909
Oil on canvas, 96.5 × 95 cm
Acquired 1999

The similarity between Otto Steinert's negative print of a **Black Nude** (Schwarzer Akt) and Ernst Ludwig Kirchner's wooden **Standing Girl** (Stehendes Mädchen) figure is impressive. Of course the limbs seem much more sculptural in the negative image, particularly when the contrast between black and white in the body is further emphasised by a white background.

Kirchner's work is one of numerous carved wooden figures, along with many wooden sticks, that the artist made in the evenings when the light was no longer good enough to paint by. The subject is probably Gerda

OTTO STEINERT
* 1915 Saarbrücken † 1978 Essen
Black Nude, 1958
Gelatine silver negative,
60.3 × 45.6 cm
Acquired 1979

ERNST LUDWIG KIRCHNER
* 1880 Aschaffenburg † 1938 Frauenkirch
Standing Girl, 1913/14
Wood, painted, 44 cm
Acquired 1992

Schilling, the sister of Kirchner's partner Erna. It is perfectly plausible that this nude figure was created during Kirchner's summer stay on Fehmarn. Kirchner spent some of the summer months there with his 'models' from 1912 onwards, Erna and sometimes Gerda. Friends like Otto Müller and his wife Maschka also visited Kirchner and were immediately immortalised in art. This little wooden figure, small and unusually finely and evenly worked by Kirchner, could date from 1913 or 1914. The reticent use of colour, to bring out Gerda's hair-do, was typical of Kirchner, and also of Heckel. In 1914, on another summer visit to

Fehmarn, Kirchner had to leave the island prematurely because of the outbreak of the First World War. This street scene, probably the last one, was produced when he got back to Berlin. Kirchner captures the bustle of Leipziger Strasse in central Berlin in much more detail than usual. Tram, street lamps, neon signs and lively activity under the shopping arcades convey modern life in the big city. Two women dressed up to the nines, presumably the coquettes who people Kirchner's street pictures, are seen strolling on the right-hand side, followed by a pair of elegantly dressed men wearing top hats. *vL*

ERNST LUDWIG KIRCHNER
Leipziger Strasse with Electric Tram, 1914
Oil and mixed technique on canvas,
71.2 × 87 cm
Acquired 1981

Around 1910, the Brücke artists were
seized by the fascination of the exotic.
Nolde had had the same idea, even
though he had long ceased to be a
member of the group. The model of
'primitive' art helped him, like the
others, to turn back to natural, original
objects and use fetishes, masks and cult
figures to heighten the expressive quality
of his work. Nolde started to investigate
the collection in the Berlin Ethnological
Museum intensively in 1910, recording
it in countless sketches. The first painting based on a preliminary drawing of
an African figure is **Still Life with Wooden
Figure** (Stilleben mit Holzfigur). In
1913/14, the opportunity finally arose
to travel to the South Seas. Here Nolde
probably saw numerous wooden figures
like the **Malanggan** ones. In 1915, a
considerable South Sea collection even
reached the Folkwang Museum through
his good offices. The artefacts did not

EMIL NOLDE
* 1867 Nolde † 1956 Seebüll
In the Café, 1911
Oil on canvas, 73 × 89 cm
Acquired 1957

PAPUA NEW GUINEA
Malanggan cult figure, 19C
Wood, painted, 108 cm
Acquired by Karl Ernst Osthaus in 1915

interest him in the context of the rites they were produced for, but simply as stimuli for his own painterly output. Another focus of Nolde's interest was the whole dubious nature of life in large cities. Disturbed relationships between people are revealed in **café** and street scenes. Such themes become metaphors and symbols of man's alienation in the city. Nolde reports on the hectic quality of life: 'My pictures produced from observations and on the spot drawings this winter were different from what came before and after. They … all used strong light and colour contrasts, capturing the unusual and elegant characters sharply and for a moment in time.' Nolde was concerned to show the fleeting euphoria of superficial brilliance, the eeriness of a world reflecting feigned happiness. *Fro*

EMIL NOLDE
Still Life with Wooden Figure, 1911
Oil on canvas, 77 × 65 cm
Acquired by Karl Ernst Osthaus c. 1912, confiscated in 1937, reacquired 1994

1910 found the Brücke style at its high point. The works have an aesthetic of their own, one that cannot be measured in terms of earlier styles. **Standing Child** (Stehendes Kind) clearly demonstrates the

rejection of detailed intricacy. The drawing thrives on the effect of the two-dimensional shapes, along with the powerful colour contrasts between black, green and red, plus the white of the unprinted paper. The irregular white lines that separate some of the colours from each other are a result of the printing process. Heckel did not print from several blocks, but sawed up the finished long timbers, coloured the individual parts and put them back together again for printing. This printing process emphasises the two-dimensional quality of the colour, their powerful intensity and the contrast between the figure and the abstract pictorial background. Colour is not used to determine the material of the objects or to describe material. Instead it emphasises its own sensual quality, and is oriented towards overall effect. Schmidt-Rottluff took a further step towards stylisation, particularly in the women's heads produced after 1915. The features of the **Girl from Kowno** (Mädchen aus Kowno) were built up tectonically and can be traced back to stereometric forms. The hardened, robust formal language, including parallel hatching intended to make a tactile effect, shows the profound influence of African art, of the kind seen in the **Baule mask**. The slit eyes and the small mouth are comparable with the mask from Africa's central Ivory Coast, and so is the precisely cut oval form of the face with the parallel profiling of the hair. *Fro*

AFRICA, IVORY COAST
Baule mask
Wood, 23 × 15 cm
Acquired by Karl Ernst Osthaus in 1916

PAPUA NEW GUINEA
Ceremonial shield
Keram River, lower Sepik area
Wood, painted, 111 cm
Acquired by Karl Ernst Osthaus in 1915

KARL SCHMIDT-ROTTLUFF
∗ 1884 Chemnitz † 1976 Berlin
Girl from Kowno, 1918
Woodcut, 50.3 × 39 cm
Acquired 2004

ERICH HECKEL
∗ 1883 Döbeln † 1970 Radolfzell
Standing Child, 1910
Coloured woodcut, 37.5 × 27.7 cm
Acquired 1964

HANNAH HÖCH
* 1889 Gotha   † 1978 Berlin
Sweetie, 1926 (from the *From an Ethnographic Museum* series)
Collage, 30 × 15.5 cm
Acquired 1993

ironic judgment on the Expressionists' world-weary move to primitivism. Ethnographic rawness is contrasted with European grace in her collage. None of the Expressionists enthusing about the primitive figures from the Ethnographic Museum would ever have wanted to swap his **sweetie** (Die Süsse) for this archaic idol. *vL*

The crude and powerful lines of dancer Sidi Reha look as though they are carved in wood. Heckel shapes the collapsed, **tired**-looking torso of his wife with deep furrows in her cheeks. Sidi is lying in bed almost upright, and completely exhausted. By using agitated painting gestures and choosing glowing colours, Heckel succeeds in imbuing the picture with suffering and tension. The vitality of the archaically block-like, coarsely carved **Crouching Woman** (Hockende) comes from her ambiguous pose and the suggestion that she is a caryatid carrying a load and is also a female nude. The naked woman huddles with her head thrust slightly forwards, her right hand on her temple and her left hand on the back of her head. Like Kirchner, Heckel colours the hair and the plinth black. Analogies between the painting and the sculpture suggest that Sidi might also have been the model for the crouching woman. Dadaist Hannah Höch delivers an

RICH HECKEL
1883 Döbeln † 1970 Radolfzell
Tired, 1913
Portrait of Sidi Heckel
Oil on canvas, 81 × 70.5 cm
Acquired 1996

ERICH HECKEL
Crouching Woman, 1912
Lime-wood, painted, 30 cm
Acquired 1999

Schmidt-Rottluff use powerful, typical brushstrokes placed close together to portray the buildings and countryside on the Curonian Spit on the coast of East Prussia. Brightly coloured, spontaneous, reducing the pictorial subjects to their basic statements, was the style the painter used at this time. Erich Heckel seems to approach the theme of landscape even more radically. This scene of Walkers (Spaziergänger) strolling beside Grunewald lake and painted in Berlin is among his first pictures. Branches on the black tree-trunks gesticulate wildly in front of the blue of the water and the green of the bushes in the background, underlining the essentially Fauvist character of his painting at the time. The view through tangled trees into the landscape opening up behind seems to have fascinated Steinert as well. The typically hard black-and-white contrast set up by the photographer, rather like a pen and ink drawing, increases the abstract effect. *v*

KARL SCHMIDT-ROTTLUFF
* 1884 Chemnitz † 1976 Berlin

Curonian Spit, Nidden/Nida, 1914
Mixed technique on canvas, 87 × 101 cm
Acquired 1974

RICH HECKEL
1883 Döbeln † 1970 Radolfzell

Walkers by the Lake, 1911
Tempera on canvas, 71 × 81 cm
Acquired 1956

OTTO STEINERT
* 1915 Saarbrücken † 1978 Essen

Trees in Solfatare, 1964
Gelatine silver, 59.3 × 48.8 cm
Acquired 1979

In the period just before the First World War, 1912/13, Ludwig Meidner painted astonishing pictures of apocalyptic landscapes, burning cities and worlds, battles at the barricades and revolutions. **Homeless People** (Heimatlose) is one of the first narratives of these dark visions full of the shattering despair to which people are brought by great misfortune.

Meidner points futuristically to the consequences that will arise from the expressively hectic pace and breathlessness of human existence in the age of technical civilisation in modern cities. Ernst Ludwig Kirchner was certainly equally affected by this development in human terms. He responded to his brie experience of war with the most

LUDWIG MEIDNER
* 1884 Bernstadt † 1966 Darmstadt
Homeless People, 1912
Burnt Out
Oil on canvas, 63 × 84 cm
Acquired 1997

GILLES PERRES
* 1946 Neuilly-sur-Seine
Mound of Corpses, 1996/97
(from the *Farewell to Bosnia* series)
Gelatine silver print, 32.4 × 48 cm
Acquired 1999

profound distress: 'I feel half dead with mental and physical torment,' he wrote to Karl Ernst Osthaus. The view of **Halle** an der Saale (Der Rote Turm) empty of human beings, where Kirchner's training company was stationed, lies in a pallid blue light, red only in the foreground, lighting the streets like molten iron flowing into the abyss. The balls of cloud rising out of the background indicate the approaching artillery. The apocalypse Meidner presents could not turn out any more vividly than it does in the case of the fallen soldiers photographed by Gilles Perres, whose picture of **corpses** in Bosnia shocked the world in recent times. *vL*

ERNST LUDWIG KIRCHNER
∗ 1880 Aschaffenburg † 1938 Frauenkirch
The Red Tower in Halle, 1915
Tempera on canvas, 120 × 90.5 cm
Acquired 1953

Biblical themes or legends of the saints regularly inspired Emil Nolde to produce whole groups of works. A member of the Brücke circle for a year, Nolde uses powerful formal distortions and expressively applied colour to narrate the legend of **St. Mary of Egypt** (Heilige Maria von Ägypten), whose corpse was to be buried by St. Zosimus. Zosimus was too weak, and asked God for help, who sent the lion to dig the grave. Nolde adds the familiar floral world of his home to the events in the desert, to make the air of strangeness even more powerful. Here as in the picture **Except Ye Become as Little Children** (So Ihr Werdet Nicht wie Kinder), it is the colours that symbolise the subject matter and ultimately the whole spiritual statement. The allegory

EMIL NOLDE
∗ 1867 Nolde † 1956 Seebüll
St Mary of Egypt, 1912
Oil on canvas, 87 × 100.5 cm
Acquired 1924, confiscated in 1937, reacquired 1950

of the children allows us to anticipate the positive outcome of the story simply through the glowing shades of yellow, orange and red identifying the figure of Christ, the children, and even the apostles, despite the scepticism Nolde conveys with a brushstroke in the raised eyebrow of one of them. 'It is as though the colours loved my hands,' Nolde once said. It is this almost tangible use of colour that makes it possible to experience the world of faith in his pictures. *Kö*

EMIL NOLDE

Except Ye Become as Little Children, 1929
Oil on canvas, 120 × 106.5 cm
On loan from the Sparkassenstiftung,
Essen since 1983

The **Polish Family** shows a wishful vision in which Mueller sees himself as an Orthodox Jew. The representation of his beloved Irene Altmann as the Virgin Mary undoubtedly also alludes to her Jewish origin. She was one of his first pupils at the academy in Breslau at the beginning of 1909 and radically changed his private life. Probably for the first time, he thought of breaking up his longstanding marriage. In this picture there is also a yearning on the part of the artist for family security, which he describes with the picture of the newly born child. No birth of a child to the two of them is known of, but the poodle lurking under the bench, called Heiko, was a faithful companion of the first years in Breslau. The difference in religions made

OTTO MUELLER
∗ 1874 Liebau † 1930 Breslau
Polish Family, 1919
Distemper on hessian, 179.5 × 112 cm
Acquired 1952

marriage inadvisable. In the same year, Mueller also painted his wife **Maschka** in this very self-assured attitude with the critical glare. On the wall behind is a mask with closed eyelids. The mask—comparable with a **mbuya mask**—has the features of the artist.

Despite their divorce in 1921 and a turbulent existence thereafter, he remained in close touch with Maschka for the rest of his life. *vL*

AFRICA, ZAIRE
West Pende *mbuya* mask
Wood, 19.5 × 16.5 cm
Acquired by Karl Ernst Osthaus in 1916

OTTO MUELLER
Maschka with Mask, 1919
Distemper on hessian, 95.5 × 67.5 cm
Acquired 1978

Norwegian painter Edvard Munch found a place in the collection at a very early stage. Osthaus bought a first painting as early as 1903, and the Folkwang mounted its first Munch exhibition in 1906. But three more paintings by the artist and graphic works were confiscated by the Nazis in 1937. The paintings that are to be found in the Folkwang today, the Winter Landscape

with Stars and *Summer Night. The Lonely Ones*, and a panel from the frieze of twelve paintings that Max Reinhardt, director of the Deutsches Theater, commissioned for the Berlin Kammerspiele in 1906/07, are thus purchases dating from the fifties and sixties respectively. In the eighties the collection managed to acquire the Boy Bathing, a monumental work by Munch.

EDVARD MUNCH
* 1863 Löiten † 1944 Ekely
Winter Landscape with Stars, 1901
Oil on canvas, 59.5 × 74 cm
Acquired 1954

EDVARD MUNCH
Boy Bathing, 1910/11
Oil on canvas, 201 × 96 cm
Acquired 1984

It was painted in summer 1907, after he had been ill for a long time. The boy stands in front of a horizontally structured background on the Baltic beach, powerful but perhaps also a little stiff and academic-looking. This is the left-hand panel of a triptych painted directly from nature, *Men on the Beach*, depicting the three ages of man. *vL*

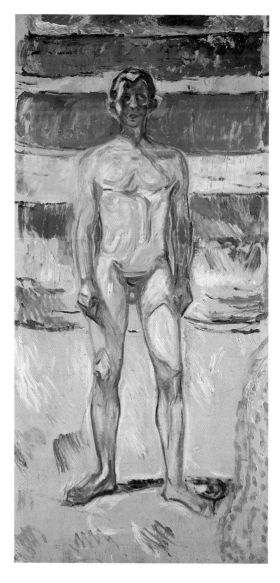

Oskar Kokoschka met **Alma Mahler**, the widow of the musician Gustav Mahler, in 1912. He loved her tempestuously and ultimately unhappily until 1914. The **double portrait**, in which there is no contact between either eyes or hands, is, along with the many other paintings and drawings of the artist's beloved, evidence of a fervent but conflict-ridden passion. Alma Mahler must have been irresistibly attractive to the 'lords of creation'. After separating from Kokoschka in 1915 she married the architect Walter Gropius, and finally emigrated to California in the United States with author Franz Werfel. In 1919 Kokoschka was appointed to the Dresden Academy of Fine Arts. Before leaving there in 1924 he produced a series of views of the city, including this **Elbe Landscape**. (Elblandschaft).
A putto on the roof of the college steers the viewer's eye along the Elbe, over the Augustusbrücke and Marienbrücke bridges to the Lösnitz Hills. We see the Elbe warehouses on the left and St Jacobi's church, the tower of the

OSKAR KOKOSCHKA
* 1886 Pöchlarn † 1980 Montreux
Double Portrait, 1912/13
Double Portrait
Oil on canvas, 100 × 90 cm
Acquired 1976

HELLEN VAN MEENE
* 1972 Alkmaar
Untitled, 2003
(from the *Folkwang 2003* series)
C-Print, 38.5 × 38.5 cm
Acquired 2003

Ostragehege slaughterhouse in the middle and finally the buildings in Dresden New Town on the right bank of the Elbe.

Hellen van Meene chooses the look out of the picture even more directly than Kokoschka for her **untitled** double portrait of two young girls. A random moment, it would seem, and yet capturing the outward gaze with complete concentration, attracting attention. *vL*

OSKAR KOKOSCHKA
Elbe Landscape in Dresden, 1923
Oil on canvas, 65.5 × 95.7 cm
Acquired 1951

OSKAR KOKOSCHKA
Alma Mahler, 1912
Charcoal, 49.1 × 34.5 cm
Acquired pre-1929

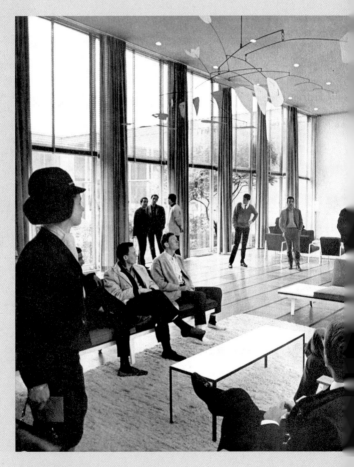

Folkwang Museum, Essen,
Garden Room, post-1960

'The question of whether contemporary art is in its heyday or in the run-up to it can scarcely be answered from where we are now.
Our acceptance or rejection does not make it either better or worse. But as long as it is asking questions or being questioned, it seems to me in any case to be one possible way of determining the position of humanity in our labyrinthine times, even when there is not always an answer to be found.'

Paul Vogt, 1981

The development of Cubism is essentially a pioneering achievement by two artists—Pablo Picasso and Georges Braque. A pictorial invention based on Paul Cézanne, using subtle control of light and a wealth of textures and materials, Cubism increasingly distanced itself from pictorial narrative to become a temporary distortion of all pictorial themes. Objects used fragmentarily in the process anticipated abstraction as the approach developed into Analytical Cubism. The three examples from the collection presented here are part of this transitional stage. Typical of Léger, Braque and Mondrian are the constantly recurring, basic features in their still lifes and landscapes that provide an artificial element of detachment in various ways. Thus the letters STAL in Braque's still life **Bottle and Newspaper** (Bouteille et Journal) are a reminder of the southern French newspaper *Réveille Postal*, while Mondrian's **Composition X** marks his path from traditional landscape painting via the analysis of a tree structure systematised here to

FERNAND LÉGER
* 1881 Argentan   † 1955 Gif-sur-Yvette
Houses under the Trees, 1913
Les Maisons sous les Arbres
Oil on canvas, 55 × 46 cm
Acquired 1959

his final embracing of complete
abstraction. Meantime, Léger's curved
forms and surfaces in his **houses**
(Les Maisons sous les Arbres) seem
Cubist for as long as one pays
attention to their borderlines. They
seem flatter when the entwined
figures and interrelated colour and
formal values are in the foreground.
vL

GEORGES BRAQUE
1882 Argentan-sur-Seine
1963 Paris

Bottle and Newspaper, 1911/12
Bouteille et Journal
Oil on canvas, 72.5 × 59.5 cm
Acquired 1962

PIET MONDRIAN
∗ 1872 Amersfoort † 1944 New York

Composition X, 1912/13
Apple Tree
Oil on canvas, 65.5 × 75.5 cm
Acquired 1957

'…we both love blue, horses for Marc, riders for me. So the name invented itself.' (Kandinsky) Intensive artistic discussions in the early 20th century in Munich provided the intellectual background to the Blauer Reiter (Blue Rider) group of artists. The name was originally coined for the legendary art almanac with art contributions and reviews that appeared in 1912. The appearance of the first issue was delayed by planning for the exhibition of the same name. Together they expressed an idea—a very personal achievement by two kindred artist spirits—Vassily Kandinsky and Franz Marc. Franz Marc's painting **Horse in the Landscape** (Pferd in der Landschaft) was painted not far from the upper Bavarian village of Sindelfingen. For Marc, animals in the landscape were a bridge between life and nature, a way to recreate their lost unity. For only animals had retained their purity, their 'chaste majesty', as Marc called it. Highly romantic, in a way evocative of Caspar David Friedrich's *Mann über dem Nebelmeer* (Man above the Sea of Mist), the horse, with its back

FRANZ MARC
∗ 1880 Munich † 1916 Verdun

Horse in the Landscape, 1910
Oil on canvas, 85 × 112 cm
Acquired 1953

to the viewer, looks out at the rolling
Alpine foothills. Not far from here,
Kandinsky and Gabriele Münter had
discovered the little market town of
Murnau—a place with a magnificent
Baroque church whose striking
tower also features in the **Landscape
with Church** (Landschaft mit Kirche).
Kandinsky justified dissolving
representational relationships in Expressionist abstraction in his published
essay *On the Spiritual Content of Art*.
Kandinsky's—and Marc's—idea,
characterised by dualism and a profoundly religious quality, of creating
painting from the impetus of 'inner
necessity', his notion of making the
'great spiritual quality' and 'inner sound'
of his thoughts visible in pictorial
invention, was scarcely understood even
by his closest friends, and 'abstraction'
reduced to colours was at times
dismissed by critics as 'decoration'. *vL*

VASSILY KANDINSKY
∗ 1866 Moscow † 1944 Neuilly-sur-Seine
Landscape with Church, 1913
Oil on canvas, 78 × 100 cm
Acquired 1962

Kandinsky invited Robert Delaunay to take part in the Blauer Reiter exhibition in Munich. Simultaneously with the city pictures he showed there, Delaunay was working on his **Eiffel Tower** series, which he called 'destructive' and which indicate his allegiance to Cubism, though with highly individual colouring.

Labelled 'Orphism' by Apollinaire, the vaunted transformation of the 'reduced palette' of Braque's and Picasso's Cubism into crystalline, transparent colour painting was intense and at the same time influential on contemporary artists and modernism. Delaunay was seeking to realise a kind

ROBERT DELAUNAY
* 1885 Paris † 1941 Montpellier
Eiffel Tower, 1910/11
Tour Eiffel
Oil on canvas, 130 × 97 cm
Acquired 1964

of autonomous painting, largely
pursuing an ordering of colour and its
contrastes simultanés that also adhered
to the harmonious intervals and rhythms
of the outside world in order to achieve
a sense of creating space on the flat
surface. 'Simultaneous contrasts,' said
Delaunay, 'secure the dynamics of the
colours and their structure in the picture;
they are the strongest expressive device
for reality.'
Alexander Archipenko also put this idea
into practice in his tension-filled untitled
figurine assembled from convex and
concave colour forms. *vL*

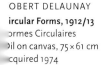

OBERT DELAUNAY
ircular Forms, 1912/13
ormes Circulaires
)il on canvas, 75 × 61 cm
cquired 1974

ALEXANDER ARCHIPENKO
✳ 1887 Kiev † 1964 New York
Untitled, c. 1916/17
Plaster, coloured, painted, 40 cm

Despite his obvious enthusiasm for Delaunay, August Macke responded reticently at first, and then also in an appropriately different way from his friend Franz Marc, who started as early as 1912/13 to break his paradisiacal animal and landscape pictures up prismatically. Macke kept some of the same subject matter while taking up ideas from Delaunay's series for reordering his pictorial world. He obviously continued to revisit the colour field painting and pictorial structures of Delaunay's window pictures and, as can be seen from the Milliner's Shop (Hutladen), alternated between more or less geometrically organised colour fields that determined

PAUL KLEE
∗ 1879 Münchenbuchsee † 1940 Muralto
Moonrise (St Germain), 1915, 242
Watercolour and pencil on paper on card,
18.4 × 17.2/17.5 cm
Acquired 1958

FRANZ MARC
∗ 1880 Munich † 1916 Verdun
Recumbent Bull, 1913
Gouache/tempera on paper, 40 × 46 cm
Acquired 1967

the structure of the picture over and beyond the shapes involved in the representational quality he retains. Macke's subjects remain more committed to representation—the Bonn artist approached the layering and fragmentation of representational shapes typical of Delaunay only to a limited extent. Just as Franz Marc effectively inscribed and almost dissolved his Recumbent Bull (Liegender Stier) in the French artist's Cubist grid, Paul Klee is also not free of Delaunay's pictorial system in his watercolour of Moonrise (St. Germain) (Mondaufgang, St. Germain), painted during his journey to Tunis in 1914. *vL*

AUGUST MACKE
∗ 1887 Meschede † 1914 in action in Champagne

Milliner's Shop, 1914
Oil on canvas, 60.5 × 50.5 cm
Acquired by Karl Ernst Osthaus pre-1921, confiscated in 1937, reacquired 1953

Marc's adoption of Delaunay's compositional principles is striking, in his prismatic faceting within the arrangement,
for example. **Below** we have Marc's
sensual, abstract poetic approach,
imbued with spiritual light and mystic
harmony, **above**, Delaunay's view out
of the window of the modern metropolis
by the Seine with the Eiffel Tower and big
wheel, oscillating between abstraction

ROBERT DELAUNAY
* 1885 Paris † 1941 Montpellier
Windows on the Town, 1912
Les Fenêtres sur la Ville
Oil on canvas, 53 × 207 cm
Acquired 1966

and representation. Delaunay, for all his prismatic dissolution, shows his enduring down-to-earth nature and the enthusiasm for the achievements of modern technology he shared with the Futurists. Franz Marc on the other hand tries to distance himself from shaped motifs and effectively to dynamise subject matter and space and translate them into an ecstatic world. *vL*

FRANZ MARC
1880 Munich † 1916 Verdun
Shapes Playing, 1914
Spielende Formen
Mixed technique on canvas, 65.5 × 170 cm
Acquired 1976

This **Nubiola Portrait**, a three-quarter-length with table, is one of the artist's early works, before he turned to Surrealism and found his own characteristic style. The figure, presented in vigorous curves despite the seated position, contrasts with the Cubist forms of table and carpet. Reminiscent of prisms, these cubes are evidence of Miró's coming to terms with the Cubism that his fellow-countryman Picasso had developed with Georges Braque in Paris a few years earlier. The colourful quality of the painting and the coarsened stylisation of Cubist formal idiom suggest another possible source, however. The old Moorish-Spanish tradition of **tile tableaux** still survived in the Iberian peninsula and found its final apotheosis

JOAN MIRÓ
* 1893 Barcelona † 1983 Palma de Mallorca
Nubiola Portrait, c. 1917
Oil on canvas, 104 × 113 cm
Acquired 1966

in the buildings of Miró's great model Antonio Gaudí, and this seems to be responsible for the prismatic, splintered forms in his painting. Forming patterns with triangles and an accumulation of identical arcs and straight lines is found in both the tile tableaux and the shapes on the tables and carpet in Miró's painting. In his search for new expressive forms, the Catalan painter combines the ancient techniques of Spanish tile painters with the Cubist formal language that had just established itself in the French capital. The synthesis of old and new, applied and free art created an impressive work full of power and independence from this artist, who was still a young man. *HG*

ANDALUSIA
Tile tableau from the Alcázar
in Niebla, 15 C
Cuerdaseca, 57 × 80.2 cm
Acquired by Karl Ernst Osthaus c. 1910

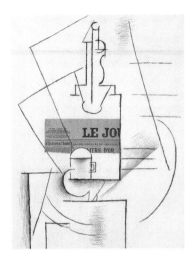

PABLO PICASSO
∗ 1881 Málaga † 1973 Mougins

Bottle, Cup and Newspaper, 1912
Bouteille, Tasse, Journal
Collage/charcoal on paper, 63 × 48 cm
Acquired 1961

LYONEL FEININGER
∗ 1871 New York † 1956 New York

Mellingen, 1915
Church Tower
Oil on canvas, 100 × 80 cm
Acquired 1998

Basing himself on the work of Cézanne, Picasso analysed the pictorial subject in his Cubist still life with a few lines in a scene that retains its two-dimensional quality. The collaged newspaper cutting in **Bottle, Cup and Paper** (Bouteille, Tasse, Journal) is intended to reconnect the pictorial presentation, already very abstract, with reality. Feininger, who later taught at the Bauhaus, concentrates on characteristic geometrical elements in his city views. Starting with Cubism, he developed formal structural elements that sometimes acquire a very expressive quality. In this way, Feininger's church tower composition in **Mellingen** comes astonishing close to the structure of Picasso's drawing. His colleague Moholy-Nagy, an all-round design genius, shaped the Bauhaus's new direction in uniting technology and art. Geometrical forms and filigree bodies maintain a floating equilibrium in his pictures (e.g. **A VIII**), indicating the search for a perfect balance between emotion and intellect in the age of technology. Germaine Krull's eye for the **Eiffel Tower** in Paris was trained by such Constructivist abstract images. But her unusual perspective on the iron stays shows that she is still able to invent her own aesthetic images. *HN*

LÁSZLÓ MOHOLY-NAGY
* 1895 Bácsborsód † 1946 Chicago
A VIII, 1923
Oil on canvas, 95 × 77 cm
Acquired 1971

GERMAINE KRULL
* 1897 Wilda † 1985 Wetzlar
Eiffel Tower, 1928
(from the *Métal* series)
Gelatine silver print, 22.6 × 15.2 cm
Acquired 1995

In the 1920s the genre portrait was subjected to innovative artistic strategies. Concern about being and essence thrust the artistic subject between the model and the image more insistently than ever.

Sander's **Yeoman Farmer** (Herrenbauer) is just one stone from a mosaic of complex portrait studies with which he was trying to produce a social documentary picture compendium of his day. Dix's anonymous pair of artistes from the *Circus* series on the other hand invoke the themes of Eros and death. The drawing derives its drama from abrupt, angular lines, the outward-facing, highly physical presentation of the couple and the repetition of the

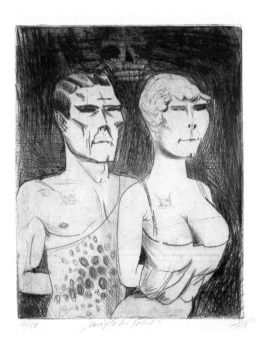

AUGUST SANDER
☀ 1876 Herdorf an der Heller † 1964 Cologne

Yeoman Farmer, c. 1925
Gelatine silver print, 23.1 × 17.6 cm
Acquired 1979

OTTO DIX
☀ 1891 Untermhaus † 1969 Singen

Despising Death, 1922
Etching, 34.5 × 27.5 cm
Acquired 1967

skull motif. The female portraits by Dix and Belling retain an element of individuality despite the stylised approach. Striking facial features gain presence from overdrawing and the reduction of details. In the **portrait** of his wife Dix uses monochrome colouring and an emphasis on the two-dimensional pictorial surface for the structural treatment of the media qualities of his own métier, while Belling opts for an accentuated compilation of abstract formal elements, which impressively tie the reflective qualities of **brass** into the overall effect. *PS*

RUDOLF BELLING
* 1886 Berlin † 1972 Krailing

Brass Head, 1925
Portrait of Toni Freeden
Brass, 38 cm
Acquired 2003

OTTO DIX

Portrait of Mrs Martha Dix, 1928
Mixed technique on wood, 60 × 59.5 cm
Acquired 1969

MAX ERNST
* 1891 Cologne † 1976 Paris

The Emperor of Wahaua, c. 1920
Oil on canvas, 83.5 × 78 cm
Acquired 1972

AFRICA, NIGERIA
Benin head, first half of 18C
Brass, iron inlay, 31.5 cm,
Ø of the plinth, 29 cm
Acquired 1932 [Kunstsammlungen, Essen]

Adopting free form, Max Ernst collaged the photograph of King Daudi from Emil Ludwig's book *Die Reise nach Afrika* along with paraphrased shapes from the world of botany, which the artist discovered in a teaching aids catalogue for schools in 1919, into his painting of **The Emperor of Wahaua**, dated c. 1920. At that time the Surrealists were greatly fascinated by remote Africa, its inhabitants and their rituals, which they combined with their own ideas of magic, longing and subconscious sensations to create Surrealist effects. It is not just King Daudi's fixedly staring eyes that give us a sense of something that cannot quite be pinned down; the same is true of the eyes of the **king's head** from Benin. We have to imagine a large elephant's tusk in the hole at the top of the head. The high collar, made of tiny coral tubes, and two *ikao*, signs of sacrificial blood on the forehead as insignia of a magic rite, were considered signs of kingly power. Thus the head symbolizes the idea of quasi-divine rule, not least because of the penetrating eyes. *Kö*

Belling's **Sculpture 23** (Skulptur 23) can stand as probably the most successful embodiment of the programme for the new sculpture he formulated in the previous year. It was intended to be a synthesis of sculpture and space, with the sculptural material body and the immaterial 'spatial body' having equal status. Despite his geometrically structured forms, Belling saw himself as being in the tradition of Baroque sculpture, which ultimately was about combining sculptural bodies and spatial bodies to make a formal virtuoso whole. The sculptor dedicated the colour pencil drawing **Head** (Kopf) to his friend Carl Einstein, who in 1924 described the sculpture of a head as a three-dimensional structure in air

RUDOLF BELLING
∗ 1886 Berlin † 1972 Krailing

Sculpture 23, 1923
(Skulptur 23)
Brass-bronze, 40.5 cm
Acquired 1969

RAOUL HAUSMANN
∗ 1886 Vienna † 1971 Limoges

Mechanical Games, 1957
Gelatine silver, copy montage,
30.4 × 40 cm
Acquired 1979

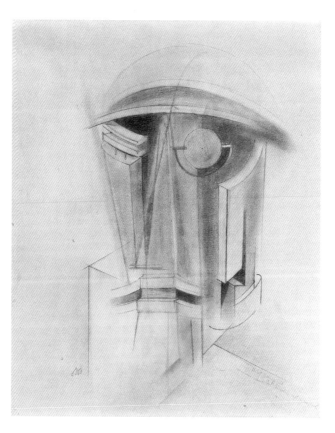

and material form. The sculpture acquires its 'three-dimensional contrast' from its contrasting juxtapositions and combinations, and 'mass is attuned into a multiple spatial game'. Belling's tectonic head was probably a response to Raoul Hausmann's *Mechanical Head* of 1919, shown at the Berlin DADA Fair. The Dadaist envisaged this wooden head used by wigmakers as a mirror to hold up to his contemporaries, whose faces he saw as nothing but images made by hair-

dressers. This wooden head recurs in Hausmann's 1957 multiple exposure **Mechanical Games** (Jeux Mécaniques) combined with two wooden jointed dolls, emphasizing the mechanical qualities of a modern lifestyle. But now the technical applications of the Dada period and the contemporary critical message associated with them are being suppressed in favour of mythologising the heads. *HG*

RUDOLF BELLING
Head, 1923
Colour pencils, lead pencil, 40 × 32.4 cm
Acquired 2004

The Surrealists felt that reality was not enough, they had to add in the wondrous, the inscrutable, the imaginary and the subconscious as well. They looked for presentation methods that included the random aspect of art production, cutting out the element of rational control during the creative process. André Masson used the inspiration of *écriture automatique* for his paintings, which abandoned themselves entirely to the imagination. He created associative pictorial worlds reminiscent of labyrinths, like the painting **The Crown** (Die Krone). This depiction of signs and symbol seems like a still life, and according to Masson illustrates the struggle of life against death.

Photography, which according to André Breton refers to 'the image as produced in automatic writing', was a popular expressive medium for the Surrealists. Photography without a camera in particular contained creative potential for the photographers, because it was possible to include a random element as an essential creative feature. Various ways of changing negatives or the exposure process offered the Surrealist photographers a broad experimental field. Roger Parry's photography combined the techniques of the photogram and the chemigram. He distributed fragile paper shapes and liquid over the light-sensitive layer of the photographic paper, and then exposed it. In this way Parry brought abstract scenery into being that had never existed in reality, as in the untitled picture here, thus also picking up the Surrealist idea of the *objet trouvé*. The fluid formal transitions in both pictures convey a

ROGER PARRY
* 1905 Paris   † Paris 1977
Untitled, 1929
Gelatine silver, 11.6 × 17.5 cm
Acquired 1990

sensation of shapes perpetually
emerging and dissolving, and also the
metamorphosis of the representational
into the non-representational. *KK*

ANDRÉ MASSON
1896 Balangy-sur-Thérain † 1987 Paris

The Crown, 1924
La Couronne
Oil on canvas, 92 × 73 cm
Acquired 1969

The Catalan Surrealist's work trans-
forms the Mediterranean coastal landscape into a place of sexual encounter.
Everything seems to be aching with desire
for union, under a fiery-red sky. The
white, prone body of the beach stretches
its thigh out to the blue water. A phallus
rises out of the earth's lap. On the horizon
an enormous plant thrusts up into the
sky. Its clover-leaf pistil seems like a
monstrous female sexual organ, for
which Miró found models in primeval
rock drawings and 'primitive art' sculptures. This honey-yellow flower pistil,
opening itself up for fertilisation, has
just attracted a (male) fly, but this is
immediately snapped up by a (female)
bird. Miró sees women as both a sweet
temptation and as threatening to
swallow him whole. The painting shows
its formal affinities with the millennia-
old clay vessel in the shape of a zebu not
only in the contrast of the organically
swelling curves with the pointed horns.
In its ritual function for the cult of the
dead, the animal vessel embodies and

accompanies the transition from life
to death as a grave gift—a subject that
the eroticised landscape touches on as
well. *HG*

IRAN, MARLIK CULTURE
**Clay vessel in the shape of a zebu,
late 2nd millennium BC**
Clay, 26 cm
Acquired 1963

JOAN MIRÓ
☆ 1893 Barcelona   † 1983 Palma de Mallorca
Landscape, 1924/25
Paysage
Oil on canvas, 69.5 × 64.5 cm
Acquired 1971

Stimulated by his contacts with the New York Dadaists and Paris Surrealists, American photographer Man Ray sought new expressive possibilities, and worked with a number of experimental photographic procedures. He used photograms as well as photomontage to detach the subject from its usual context and question the objectivity of the familiar world of appearances.

In his portrait photograph, Man Ray makes **Dora Maar**'s face stand out from its surroundings through the unusual positive-negative treatment of partial solarisation. The pair of hands placed at chin level conjures up the history and symbolism of the hand motif in art. At the same time it reminds us of Maar's artistic activities—she was a painter and photographer and lived with Picasso in the 1940s. The portrait was presumably produced while Man Ray was on an extended stay with Picasso and other artists in Mougins in the South of France. Herbert Bayer also saw the camera as a design medium. He was a student and later also a teacher at the Bauhaus. He experimented with new perspectives and techniques for photography and established the use of new creative devices in advertising. After moving to Berlin in 1928 he worked particularly in the field of photomontage, completely changing the context by detaching individual motifs from their original surroundings. The **Lonely City Dweller** (Einsamer Grossstädter) is an immediate presence in front of a Berlin façade

MAN RAY
∗ 1890 Philadelphia † 1976 Paris
Painter Dora Maar, 1936
Photograph, gelatine silver bromide,
partial solarisation, vintage, 22.6 × 29.4 cm
Acquired 1979

through the montage of hands and eyes — the pair of eyes set in the palms of the hands look penetratingly at the viewer, to surreal effect. *HN*

HERBERT BAYER
* 1900 Haag am Hausruck † 1985 Montecito
Lonely City Dweller, 1932
Photomontage, gelatine silver bromide,
28.5 × 23 cm
Acquired 1979

Czech photographer Hammid, born in Prague in 1907 as Alexander Hackenschmied, uses double exposure to show the silhouette of a passer-by with hat and a male face in profile outside the Madeleine in **Paris 1939**. Because the photographer's eye level is so low, the black figure stands out overwhelmingly against the light background. The photograph reverses the usual relationship between close-up and distant view: The passer-by in the foreground is in silhouette, and therefore unrecognizable, but details in the façade in the background, shown the wrong way round, can be made out easily. Hammid left Paris in 1939 and worked mainly as a film-maker in New York—the scene here is entirely reminiscent of a film still.

Belgian painter Magritte presents a similarly 'reversed' situation in his painting **The Sleepwalker** (Le Noctambule). He is walking through a café in hat and coat, while the street lamp shifts him into the street at the same time. The curtain suggests a paradoxical stage situation, where the interior is also an exterior. The sparse furnishings and the lighting make the room look cool and dark, identifying it as 'present hereafter'. Surreal presentations of space like this go back to the paintings of Giorgio de Chirico, whose pictures were a powerful influence on Magritte. Using spatial

reversals and partially absurd combinations of various everyday objects,
Magritte's Surrealist painting reveals
subconscious and traumatic elements
of the human psyche. *HN*

HAMMID
ALEXANDER HACKENSCHMIED
∗ 1907 Linz † 2004 New York
Paris 1939, 1939
Double exposure, photomontage,
24.2 × 19.2 cm
Acquired 1992

RENÉ FRANÇOIS GHISLAIN MAGRITTE
1898 Lessines † 1967 Brussels
**The Sleepwalker or the Street-Lamp,
1927/28**
Le Noctambule ou le Réverbère
Oil on canvas, 55 × 74 cm
Acquired 1977

The village church in **Gelmeroda**, not far from Weimar, is a central subject in Lyonel Feininger's work. The modest little building is stylised into a monumental cathedral here, and the architecture made into geometry in typical Feininger fashion. The pictorial architecture acquires crystalline character from the transparent-looking, glowing surfaces and the intensive use of light. Like Feininger, Florence Henri was associated with the Bauhaus, and in her **untitled 1929** picture she also fits transparent areas of glass and mirrors together to create a crystalline structure of vertical and diagonal pictorial elements. Piet Mondrian,

LYONEL FEININGER
1871 New York † 1956 New York
Gelmeroda IX, 1926
Oil on canvas, 100 × 80 cm
Acquired 1951

FLORENCE HENRI
1893 New York † 1956 New York
Untitled, 1929/30
Gelatine silver bromide, 34 × 26.7 cm
Acquired 1979

co-founder of the Dutch de Stijl movement, eliminates any connection with figurative portrayal in his strictly linear **composition**. 'So the natural forms have to be taken back to pure, unchangeable conditions,' said the artist in 1925.

While Mondrian fills his rectangular grid with the three primary colours, with which he composes ideal pictorial tones, in order to create subtly balanced conditions of equilibrium without geometry, photographer Florence Henri completes her **untitled 1928** rectangular pictorial pattern with things. Spatial relations are destabilized by changing close-up and distant views or by using mirrors. *HN*

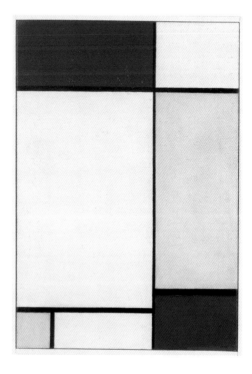

FLORENCE HENRI
Untitled, 1928
Gelatine silver bromide,
27 × 37.1 cm
Acquired 1979

PIET MONDRIAN
1872 Amersfoort
† 1944 New York
Composition with Red, Yellow, Blue, 1927
Oil on canvas, 75 × 52 cm
Acquired 1972

The myth of the origin of art goes back to a story passed on by Pliny: the daughter of potter Butades wanted to have the shadow cast by his sleeping beloved copied so her father could sculpt it in clay. The invention of photography is also based on a process that fixes the shadow of objects as a replica. But in photograms, which are contact images made without a

W.H. FOX TALBOT
☀ 1800 Melbury Abbas † 1877 Lacock

Abstraction, 1839
Photogram, 22.8 × 18.4 cm
Acquired 1961

LÁSZLÓ MOHOLY-NAGY
☀ 1895 Bácsborsód † 1946 Chicago

Untitled, Dessau, 1925–1928
Photogram, gelatine silver, 18.3 × 24.1cm
Acquired 1995

camera, the objects draw their own picture in the light—they depict themselves. In Plato's metaphor of the cave, the shadow embodies the concealed original image as a perceived copy. This is also the idea behind Asian shadow theatre. As Islam forbids figurative images, shadows were shown instead of figures—the Javanese word for 'shadow' (**wayang**) also means 'spirit'—so that their characters could be understood. The similarity between the filigree patterns of the shadow figures and Talbot's early version of the photogram (**Abstraction**) is shown to striking effect here. Both are designed to create translucency, rich internal patterning and linear precision. The form derives from the function of the shadow cast.

Bauhaus artist and teacher László Moholy-Nagy developed his photograms on a quite different basis. Unlike the other two examples, this **untitled** picture takes the form of experimental play. *DS*

JAVA

Two *wayang kulit* figures, 19C
Parchment, horn rods, r: 65 cm, l: 43.5 cm
r: Prabu Kala Juwana, prince of the Great
Raden Somba Mendanggili Empire
l: Somba, son of Kresna
Acquired by Karl Ernst Osthaus c. 1909

In ancient Greece, clay vessels like this one were placed on grave mounds as memorials. A rich variety of ornamental bands and figure friezes, thematically related to the dead person, cover the amphora with a dense carpet of different rhythmic figures, expressing the original meaning of rhythm as the order of movement in dance and circulation in a celebrating community.

LÁSZLÓ MOHOLY-NAGY
∗ 1895 Bácsborsód † 1946 Chicago
Girls' Boarding School, 1925
Collage, 48 × 30.8 cm
Acquired 1969

The removal of rhythm from life in the industrial age from the Romantic period onward led to a reassessment of rhythm in art, above all by the 20th century avant-garde. The new gods were series production and speed. Moholy-Nagy's collage with the rhythmic series of hurdlers, floor dancers and pupils at the **Girls' Boarding School** combines the photographic com-

ponents into a dynamically ornamental composition, which differs from the strict rhythmic roundelays of the Attic vase only in its modernist fragmentation and open structure. *HG*

GREECE, ATTIC
Monumental amphora with neck handles, c. 710 BC
Clay, 73 cm, Ø top: 27.8 cm, Ø belly: 35.6 cm
Acquired 1960

A dead person's survival in the here-after fuelled thought and creativity in ancient Egypt. Thus Egyptian art is full of motifs relating to the deceased's life in this world and the next. The descriptive character of these idealising motifs is particularly clear in the two-dimensional execution of this fragment of a tomb relief from Saqqara. The body of the **lady** in the tomb is modelled in considerable detail in the style of the Amarna period, which was particularly notable for its refinement in depicting human beings. The use of diagonal lines and soft curves gives the otherwise static figure feminine charm. There is a parallel in the three-dimensional statue of **Rameses II**. This

carefully executed torso is an excellent example of Egyptian sculpture's ability to represent the human form always in a more or less idealised way. The perfect condition of the portrayal stood for the perpetuation of the durability and power of men and women in their prime in the new life after death.
In Surrealism the human, mainly female, body is the starting-point for chains of thoughts and associations and thus an object much beloved of photographers. Man Ray stylised the real female body into an ancient classical torso. The white lines that run across the torso like waves of current comparable to the fluid pattern of lines in the Egyptian relief, can be seen as

EGYPT
**Torso of Rameses II, 19th dynasty,
1279–1213 BC**
Marble, 58.8 cm
Acquired by Karl Ernst Osthaus pre-1910

MAN RAY
* 1890 Philadelphia † 1976 Paris
Electricité, 1931
Photogravure, 37.7 × 27.5 cm, photogram,
copy montage
Acquired 1993

Electricité dates from 1931, and
was part of a commission for Paris's
power stations. *KK*

GYPT

ady with lotus bouquet and menit
ssumed to be from the tomb of
eneral Amaneminet of Saqqara, late
3th dynasty, Haremhab, 1319–1292 BC
imestone relief, 63 cm
cquired by Karl Ernst Osthaus in 1916

Kogan's **mask** in polished white plaster, with its closed eyes and focus on inner experiences, but also the stylised reduction of the face to the bare minimum, fits in completely with the aim of the Munich Neue Künstlervereinigung artists to combine sensations from the outside world and experiences of the inner world into a form of expression completely free of anything trivial or irrelevant (Kandinsky). Erfurth's portrait photograph of **Mary Wigman** also shows a determination to turn the eye inwards and to show spiritual turbulence through expression, the position of the head and lighting.

After the First World War, Neue Sachlichkeit (New Objectivity) was a reaction to high emotion and spiritual expression. One of its outstanding exponents was Albert Renger-Patzsch. It is not just the dangerously watchful expression on the **adder's head** (Natterkopf) that was now considered photogenic but the extreme detail, a section reducing the creature to pure form, the composition with the eye in the centre and the texture of the snake's skin, with its scales arranged to form a rhythmical pictorial pattern. The origin of art and first evidence of aesthetic sensibility are to be found in the decoration of objects with rhythmically articulated ornamental patterns of this kind, as shown by the snake and also the Chinese **funerary urn** from the pre-Christian period with its life spirals. This kind of ornamentation and patterning was used partly to make the object beautiful and partly to ward off danger. *HG*

MOISSEY KOGAN
* 1879 Orgeyev † 1943 Paris

Mask, 1912
Plaster, 23 cm
Acquired by Karl Ernst Osthaus c. 1912

HUGO WILHELM BERTHOLD ERFURTH
* 1874 Halle † 1948 Gaienhofen

Mary Wigman, 1920
Oil print, 38 × 30 cm
Acquired 1979

ALBERT RENGER-PATZSCH
∗ 1897 Würzburg † 1966 Wamel
Adder's Head, 1926
Gelatine silver, 16.9 × 28.8 cm
Acquired 1987

CHINA
**Funerary urn from the Pan-Shan area,
200 BC**
Yangshao ceramic, 36.5 cm
Acquired pre-1964

Paul Klee addressed the fundamental condition of artistic creativity. He saw pictures as genesis, not complete products. He compares artistic creativity with the natural growth process: artistic elements grow out of movement and produce forms, but without sacrificing themselves in the process. The intention behind his work is to get away from naturalistic objects and create visually pure relationships. 'Art does not reproduce the visible, but renders visible,' he said in 1920.

Ancient Walls (Altes Gemäuer) was painted while he was teaching at the Bauhaus, where he taught the theory of form and colour and later shared the free painting class with Kandinsky. This picture with its ordered and at the same time labyrinthine structure demonstrates Klee's intuitively organic and natural approach. **Fire at Full Moon** (Feuer bei Vollmond) is one of the increasingly systematised chessboard images that are still encoded symbolically. Whereas the dark colours stand for things mystical and hidden, fire alludes to the Nazi arsonists in the year they seized power, 1933.

The tendency towards networks on the pictorial surface always implies the formation of individual ciphers as well. Just as Klee invents graphic wall structures, Maclet's photograph of a wall tracks down structures and binds them into a clear pictorial composition. The Frenchman first worked as a fashion photographer for *Harper's Bazaar* and

PAUL KLEE
✳ 1879 Münchenbuchsee † 1940 Locarno-Muralto
Fire at Full Moon, 1933, 353
Watercolour on paste-paint on priming on canvas,
50 × 65 cm
Acquired 1958

Vogue in the 1920s before turning
to freelance portrait photography
and later other genres like still lifes
or landscapes. He focused on the
makeup or structure of the subject in
concentrated detailed images. The
title **Solitude** alludes to old châteaux,
but also to the feeling of loneliness.
The ancient masonry, isolated from
its original location, evokes the traces
of its history—they contain their
own secret. *HN*

PAUL KLEE
Ancient Walls (Sicily), 1924, 239
Watercolour on priming on paper on
card, 22.4 × 28 cm
Acquired 1958

DANIEL MASCLET
* 1892 Blois † 1969 Paris
Solitude, c. 1951
Gelatine silver, 39.3 × 28.5 cm
Acquired 1979

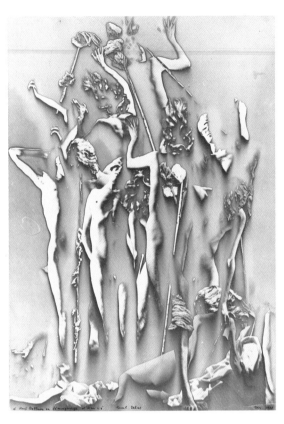

RAOUL UBAC
∗ 1910 Cologne † 1985 Dieudonné
Photo Relief, 1938
Gelatine silver, 39.6 × 27.6 cm
Acquired 1986

WILLI BAUMEISTER
∗ 1889 Stuttgart † 1955 Stuttgart
Tennis Player (in the Blue Oval), 1935
Mixed technique with sand on canvas,
backed with hardboard,
116 × 81 cm
Acquired 1961

Tanguy's **Lovers** (Les Amoureux) shows a round dance in the blue-green depths of the sea involving floating pairs of embryonic beings. Another pair comes floating by while yet another disappears into the distance. It is as though the painter had shifted the sensual motif of the garden of love into unreal, dreamlike submarine regions, in order to present it as a fantasy of the collective unconscious. In Ubac's **photorelief**, Tanguy's dream of love is transformed into the trauma of the body's boundaries (and thus its ego identity) melting away. There is a sense of the surrounding space thrusting into the female bodies and taking possession of them. Influenced by the Surrealists, Willi Baumeister also worked with organic, pneumatic structures. The sand mixed with the paint in our picture stimulates the viewer's tactile and physical senses in its interplay with the curved forms, without the body of the **Tennis Player** (Tennisspieler) being discernible anywhere. *HG*

YVES TANGUY
∗ 1900 Paris † 1955 Woodbury
The Lovers, 1929
Les Amoureux
Oil on canvas, 100 × 81 cm
Acquired 1975

A landscape in the **Empordà** region, with the bleak ruins of ancient Emporion, bleak, rocky terrain, mountains in the background, an expanse of sky— nothing unusual at a first glance, if it were not for the disturbing aspects of the almost photographic reproduction of the material and the remarkable title. The figure placed on the left, conveying the fantastic and surreal nature of the area with its 'looking for nothing' gesture, enables us to feel our way towards what the picture is saying. Dalí, as one of the leading Surrealists, breaks down the borders of perception by disguising the absurd through realistic reproduction, thus opening up new levels of meaning.

In the work by Munich court painter Kobell we are confronted with a **Bavarian landscape** near Schondorf, with remarkably placed staffage figures picked out by precisely calculated lighting effects. The horizon is set just as low as Dalí's, which makes the figures, like the apothecary, stick up into the huge sky, placed in the setting almost like set-pieces from another world. The tidy, almost swept clean landscape and the powerful shadows reinforce the impression of a stage setting in both paintings.

SALVADOR DALÍ Y DOMÉNECH
∗ 1904 Figueres † 1989 Figueres
The Empordà Apothecary Looking for Absolutely Nothing, 1936
Le Pharmacien d'Ampurdan ne Cherchant Absolument Rien
Oil and collage on wood, 30 × 52 cm
Acquired 1979

Like stage directors, Dalí and Kobell assembled their pictures from many individual studies, and elaborated the arrangement of the animals, people and earth formations into spatial planes receding into the distance: close-up, standing out against the sky like a silhouette, and then rapidly getting smaller and smaller right to the horizon. The 'fantastic' element of Kobell's atmospheric portrayal lies in the miniature-like, almost still-life execution and in the light delicacy of the colouring, which Goethe once praised as 'niceness of brush' and 'purity of colouring'. *Kö*

WILHELM VON KOBELL
∗ 1766 Mannheim † 1855 Munich

Upper Bavarian Landscape with Hunters, 1823
Landscape with Hunters near Schondorf
Oil on canvas, 44 × 63 cm
Acquired 1959

A tiny plane, close to crashing, spins through a threateningly dark sky over a little town by the sea. Radziwill's **Karl Buchstätter's Fatal Crash** (Todessturz Karl Buchstätters) was painted 17 years after the artist, an exponent of Magic Realism, watched the test pilot's fatal accident on an airfield near Bremen. This painting has a strikingly unreal atmosphere: the little town, painted with exaggerated realism, is desolate, with only a lonely hurdy-gurdy man crossing the railway line. No one seems to be taking any notice of what is happening in the sky. The composition is worked out in detail: the village street and a ditch running towards the sea lead diagonally to the vanishing point in the right half of the picture. The two level crossing barriers point up at the aeroplane like gun barrels.

If the crash symbolises a self-destructive, dehumanising devotion to technology, Andreas Gursky's panoramic photo-graph of **La Défense**, the modernistic high-rise quarter in western Paris, is particularly notable for its cold anonymity. In both pictures the leading part is played by the eloquently silent architecture, while the homeless extras perish. The imposing buildings housing multinationals, banks and insurance companies fringe a paved pedestrian area in the foreground in which very few people are moving around. Gursky photographs this urban space from a perspective that permits geometrical abstraction of the architecture photo-graphed. Whereas Radziwill's painting constitutes a sombre critique of its time, Gursky presents an apparently sober-looking stocktaking: the significance of the individual retreats when con-fronted with the built manifestations of globally active capital. *AM*

ANDREAS GURSKY
* 1955 Leipzig
La Défense, Panorama, 1987/1993
C-Print, Diasec, 73 × 150 cm
Acquired 1996

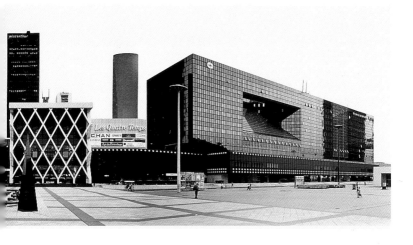

FRANZ RADZIWILL
1895 Strohausen † 1983 Wilhelmshaven

Karl Buchstätter's Fatal Crash, 1928
Canvas on hardboard, 90 × 95 cm
Acquired 1960

Danaë, mother of **Perseus**, King of Mycenae and Tiryns, asserted that he was the son of Zeus. He carried out heroic deeds appropriate to his status. His adventurous journeys brought him to the country of King Cepheus. The king's wife was so vain that she had boasted of being more beautiful than the Nereids, who complained about this to Poseidon. To save his people from punishment, Cepheus had to sacrifice his daughter Andromeda. In exchange for the girl's hand and the kingdom, Perseus rescued the royal daughter. The cook is preparing the meal, the candles have been lit, the servant has the tray

ERNST BARLACH
* 1870 Wedel † 1938 Rostock

Horror, 1923
Limewood, 90.5 cm
Acquired 1953

ready, flowers have been put out as decoration and below a chronicler with black-rimmed glasses is reading a paper. Beckmann shows this moment of triumph in discrete scenes. The scenes in the right-hand panel are also juxtaposed without direct links. The artist wanted first of all to tell the ancient story. The burning buildings, like a 'burning sea', can possibly be projected on to two time planes: antiquity, as a symbol of violence, the tragic accounts of love, murder and manslaughter in Greek and Roman mythology. But modern times as well—the German army's invasion of the Netherlands, and the burning of houses and killing of people associated with this. Beckmann as a human being (bottom right) sees the horror that is to come—the danger of being discovered himself prevents him from crying out loud in accusation. The silent gesture in Ernst Barlach's sculpture **Horror** may point in the same direction: the unspeakable nature of what has been seen. *vL*

MAX BECKMANN
∗ 1884 Leipzig † 1950 New York
Perseus, 1941
Oil on canvas, triptych,
l: 151 × 56 cm, c: 150.5 × 111 cm, r: 150.5 × 55.5 cm
Acquired 1956

Eerie bird-like creatures, heads floating in the air, strange wooden structures and an African mask take viewers of these works into a mysterious world of magic. Surrealist effects are achieved through alienation by mask-like beings, and the nocturnal, fascinating blue of the two paintings evokes dream visions. Marc Chagall's work conjures up memories of his birthplace Vitebsk, overlaying these with symbols of the

MARC CHAGALL
∗ 1889 Vitebsk † 1985 Paris

Champ de Mars, 1954/55
Oil on canvas, 149.5 × 105 cm
Acquired 1962

city of Paris and his Jewish religion, while the intertwining paths of the **Champ de Mars** fit together to form the heart symbols and connections of a new love. The power of magic is inherent in the mysterious circle of light in the Max Ernst picture, in which bird-like creatures act like **dark gods**, and also in the **kanaga mask**, which—alongside many other interpretations—symbolises the idea of unity in the

Dogon myth. Man carries the axis of the world, and the mask represents the unity and equilibrium between heaven and earth. This mask is worn during the *dama* death feast and can be read and understood only by the initiated. To anyone else it is a big bird. *Kö*

MAX ERNST
* 1891 Brühl † 1976 Paris
Dark Gods, 1957
Les Dieux Obscurs
Oil on canvas, 116 × 89 cm
Acquired 1960

AFRICA, MALI
Dogon *kanaga* mask
Wood from the kapok tree, coloured paint, wickerwork from plant fibres,
82 × 51 cm
Acquired 1958

Folkwang Museum, Essen,
View from the Stone Courtyard, 2000

'It seemed imperative to us that society and state, capital and labour should undertake everything possible for the furtherance of art in order to perfect themselves with it for the sake of mankind. —That is the position I take as in effect I return to Essen and the Folkwang Museum with a profoundly felt esteem for its history and those who created it.'

Georg W. Költzsch, 1988

After 1945, artists countered Constructive leanings with free gestural painting. In the early 1930s, after a short interlude at the Bauhaus, WOLS went to Paris, where he became an important pioneer of Tachist painting, which combines Surrealist random qualities with the subconscious in gestural improvisation. This produced a complex network of moving coloured lines and traces as a psychogram in painting. As early as 1947, Georges Mathieu stressed that these expressive resources are 'experienced'. The features of a ruined and distorted face in **Hallucinating**, scarred by delirium and inner desolation, emerge from WOLS's cocoon of coloured lines, whipped into the

WOLS
ALFRED OTTO WOLFGANG SCHULZE
* 1913 Berlin † 1951 Paris
Hallucinating, 1946/47
Oil on canvas, 81 × 81 cm
Acquired 1981

painted skin like weals or flowing over the canvas like blood.

The unequal couple in the New York streets in the **Brooklyn Dance** also seem to be hallucinating like WOLS's self-portrait. Is it the lack of focus caused by movement and the camera's wide-angle lens that makes the two passers-by look mad, or are they actually mad? The picture's refusal to answer is disturbing, and attracts attention. *HN*

WILLIAM KLEIN
∗ 1928 New York

Brooklyn Dance, 1954/55
Gelatine silver, 23.8 × 30.2 cm
Acquired 1979

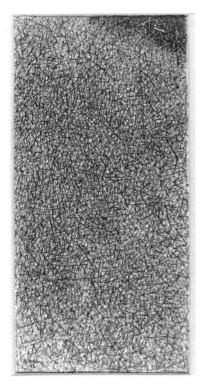

Marc Tobey applied experiences from the sphere of Zen Buddhism to the world of his pictures: meditative immersion in every trace of writing drawn by the brush, an approach of absolute concentration and slowness, the genesis of a **remote space** to be considered infinite. Delicate traces of colour flowing into each other produce a fine tissue of cosmic ideas. Likewise in Thieler's work the gesturalism of the Informel, rather like nature's creative process, suggests the creation of **dark stars** in the universe, as the title itself implies, forming images and ideas of the cosmos just from the colouring. Pollock's improvisations are produced by harnessing the expressive gestures made by his whole body. He invented a technique called 'dripping', which introduced action into his painting, a seismograph of personal psychic moods. In this kind of painting, the traditional picture space makes way for a non-perspective representation. The random elements of the dripped and sprayed colours go in every direction, and could be continued further still—on the back as well, as in this **two-sided painting**.

Callahan's piece showing **blades of grass** is contemporary with Pollock's work. It shows in the medium of photography how pictorial spaces can open up new imaginative vistas in the interaction of black-and-white contrasts. *Kö*

HARRY CALLAHAN
✷ 1912 Detroit † 1999 Atlanta
Cut, Silhouetted Blades of Grass, c. 1950
Gelatine silver, 20.3 × 25.3 cm
Acquired 1979

MARK TOBEY
✷ 1890 Centerville † 1976 Basle
Remote Space, 1962
Tempera on canvas, 100 × 50 cm
Acquired 1982

FRED THIELER
* 1916 Königsberg † 1999 Berlin

Dark Star, Fal VIII, 1961
Oil on canvas, 160 × 210 cm
Acquired 1983

JACKSON POLLOCK
* 1912 Cody † 1956 East Hampton

Two-Sided Painting, 1950/51
Oil, enamel and aluminium paint on canvas,
68.5 × 63.5 cm
Acquired 1980

FRANZ KLINE
* 1910 Wilkes-Barre † 1962 New York

Untitled, 1953/54
Oil on canvas, 170 × 208 cm
Acquired 1979

EMIL SCHUMACHER
* 1912 Hagen † 1999 Ibiza

Paracelsus, 1967
Oil, synthetic resin and assemblage on wood,
193 × 203 cm
Acquired 1972

Franz Kline was an Abstract Expressionist. The thick, heavy lines painted in the **untitled** picture in black and white look like ideograms of a psychographic nature. The raw, splintery signs embody unleashed forces, but are still restrained by the artist's mental discipline. Emil Schumacher's **Paracelsus** turns out to be brutal in a

from his own personality in his work. In 1959, he started a series of diagonal stripe pictures with slight variations. These are known as 'unfurleds', and are identified by letters of the Greek alphabet. **Ksi** consists of 13 strips of colour running irregularly across the lower corners. Here the empty canvas is seen as a positive form placed in

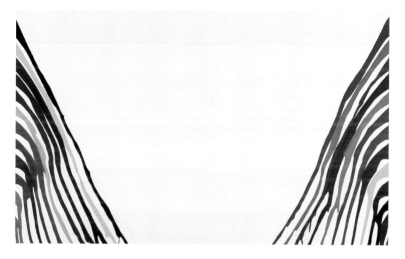

different way. In this work he had moved on from his Tachist period, during which he was able to hold his own against his contemporaries even in Paris. The influence of Informel on tactile objects like *Paracelsus* can still definitely be felt, even though a spiritual element is also making its presence felt, as the damage to the surface looks like explorations of underground realms. Whereas these images may still give us a sense of individual commitment, Morris Louis distances himself more and more

the centre, directing the colours into the corners. The unpainted canvas forms a trapezium. The colour strips are widest at the side edges, and get thinner as they move inwards and downwards. This creates an impression of flowing colour, a sensory illusion that the artist deliberately intended to create. On the other hand, the colours are arranged entirely intuitively. The viewer gains no impression of a completed picture. The sense of the incomplete underlines the openness of the form. *Fro*

MORRIS LOUIS
* 1912 Baltimore † 1962 Washington
Ksi, 1959/61
Acrylic on canvas, 264 × 438 cm
Acquired 1969

Barnett Newman chose the unusually narrow, tall format of **Prometheus Bound** for three other pictures called *Before Day, Day One* and *Ulysses* as well, thus indicating that they all belonged together.

In fact these pictures represent important steps in his development as a painter and also in theoretical terms—investigating and varying the vertical element, and then fixing colour contrasts and colour proportions. The title of our painting, as is often the case with Newman, is essentially symbolic in significance. He said that he wanted these metaphorical titles to describe his feelings at the time the painting came into being. Of course, the title of this picture, painted in the deepest black down except for the narrow strip at the bottom, triggers associations in the viewer that definitely suggest the fate of the ancient Greek hero Prometheus, who was punished by Zeus with vicious torture because he had stolen fire for mankind.

Dan Flavin uses light tubes for their original purpose. The white or fluorescent tubes in **Monument for V. Tatlin** are the working material for his art objects. Their light fields can induce a state of contemplation in viewers in the same way as Barnett Newman's paintings. *vL*

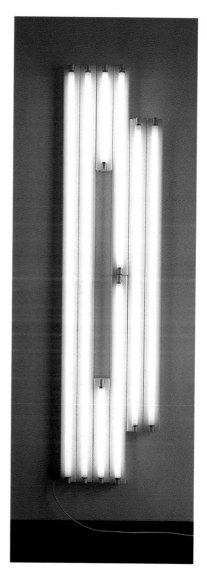

BARNETT NEWMAN
* 1905 New York † 1970 New York
Prometheus Bound, 1952
Synthetic resin on canvas, 335 × 137 cm
Acquired 1977

DAN FLAVIN
* 1933 New York † 1996 New York
Untitled (Monument for V. Tatlin), 1967
Neon tubes, white, 240 cm
Acquired 1997

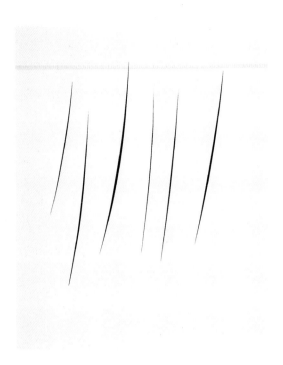

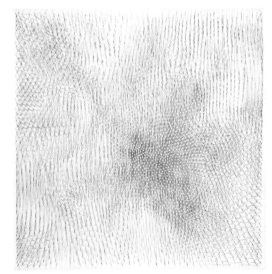

LUCIO FONTANA
∗ 1899 Rosario Santa Fé † 1968 Varese

Attese Special Idea, 1958/1965
Canvas with fabric backing,
91.5 × 73 cm
Acquired 1967

GÜNTHER UECKER
∗ 1930 Wendorf

Large White Field, 1970
Wooden frame, canvas, nails, sprayed,
150 × 150 cm
Acquired 1970

'Zero is silence. Zero is the beginning.'
Heinz Mack, Otto Piene and Yves Klein
met for the first time in Paris in 1957.
A year later, the circle widened to
include Günther Uecker and Lucio
Fontana for the first exhibition in
Piene's studio in Düsseldorf. 'Zero' is
an intellectual phenomenon attached
to a particular period, with conceptual
implications. The main representatives
of the Zero movement clearly rejected
Informel, the École de Paris, Abstract
Expressionism and any other
manifestations of this art. New expressive forms, particularly involving
the beauty of technology, led to the
triumphal progress of kinetic art,
but also to subtle forms of creative
pictorialisation. These three works
by Fontana, Piene and Uecker, based
on a white ground, culminate in
allowing both painterly and sculptural
possibilities to gain their independence.
vL

OTTO PIENE
* 1928 Laasphe

Prussian Sensibility, 1960
Sensibilité Prussienne
Oil on canvas, 100 × 130 cm
Acquired 1967

Wolf Vostell is clearly not concerned with the intelligibility of all the images that he brings together: mass-printed agency pictures of events that moved Germany. Using a Tachist gesture, Vostell overpaints his **1964** photo-collage in black, red and gold, the German national colours, effectively blurring the motif 'in order to be able to see clearly! The viewer's imagination can provide what is missing by speculating about what was there before,' said Vostell. Anselm Kiefer also veils his message, the conflict between

WOLF VOSTELL
✳ 1932 Leverkusen † 1998 Berlin
You are Leaving the American Sector, 1964
Spray paint on silk screen print on canvas photograph, 120 × 450 cm
Acquired 1994

BARBARA KLEMM
✳ 1939 Münster
West Runway Demo, Frankfurt, 1981
Gelatine silver, 27 × 39.2 cm
Acquired 1983

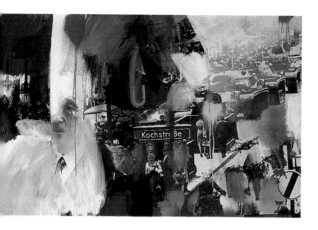

iconoclasts and iconophiles. Kiefer takes up the Byzantine **iconoclastic controversy** (Bilderstreit) of the 8th and 9th centuries and transfers it into the recent past.

The guardians of the law who had to enable the work on the **west runway** at Frankfurt Airport to start and the demonstrators who wanted to prevent it also met in hostile confrontation. Impotence and power constantly clash if human dialogue is abandoned. *vL*

ANSELM KIEFER
* 1945 Donaueschingen

Iconoclastic Controversy, 1977
Oil on canvas, 200 × 300 cm
Acquired 1982

Patches of colour of the hills in a Lofoten Island landscape in Norway moving across the picture in rhythmic flow; segments of a friendly-looking cow painted with violent brushstrokes, with split timber wedges floating in front of it; intermeshing islands of colour overlaid with a cocoon-like pattern of geological-looking rock formations like a survey—three artists at intervals of thirty years tackle one of painting's fundamental problems: the dialogue between representational form and the laws of abstract painting. The conflict between representation and abstraction in the mid-20th century—in the West, abstraction was ultimately claimed to be a sign of freedom and autonomy, while the Communist bloc stuck to representation supposedly to retain a humanitarian image of mankind—is one of modernism's most important dialogues. Ernst Wilhelm Nay, Georg Baselitz and Per Kirkeby participate in the dialogue between these two approaches through their shared principles of rhythm, layering and design. *KyZ*

PER KIRKEBY
∗ 1938 Copenhagen
Surveys the World, 1997
Oil on canvas, 300 × 500 cm
Acquired 1999

GEORG BASELITZ
∗ 1938 Deutschbaselitz

A Cow, 1968
Acrylic on canvas, 130.5 × 162.8 cm
Acquired 1986

ERNST WILHELM NAY
∗ 1902 Berlin   † 1968 Cologne

Lofoten Landscape, 1937
Oil on canvas, 105.5 × 131 cm
Acquired 1954

Ernst Wilhelm Nay was one of the most important German abstract painters in the post-war period, along with Willi Baumeister and Fritz Winter. Though the title **Of a Garden** (Eines Garten) does trigger representational associations, the genitive form leaves the viewer in a quandary. What is refers to is not is not clear. What we see is wild rhythmic forms in which the colours of a garden can be recognised but not assigned to definite objects. Less than a decade later, Nay's 'disc pictures', of which **Yellow Chromatics** (Gelbe Chromatik) is one, have a colour and formal idiom that is entirely their own. Yellow and blue confront each other in powerful chords, red and orange, pink and black weakening or strengthening the sound pattern.

Georg Baselitz, who is a good 35 years younger, chose his own way of liberating

ERNST WILHELM NAY
✳ 1902 Berlin † 1968 Cologne
Yellow Chromatics, 1960
Oil on canvas, 125 × 200 cm
Acquired 1961

ERNST WILHELM NAY
Of a Garden, 1952
Oil on canvas, 100.5 × 124.5 cm
Acquired 1952

painterly form which meant he did not have to abandon the representational world: he simply stands his pictorial motifs on their heads. So the object is retained in **Brauna**, but petty accommodations with non-artistic reality are prevented, as these would only distract us from considering the artistic qualities of the picture (the way it is painted, the composition). *KyZ*

GEORG BASELITZ
∗ 1938 Deutschbaselitz

Brauna, 1975
Oil on canvas, 250 × 200 cm
Acquired 1982

Tomlinson Court Park I is part of a 21-part series of black stripe pictures. Frank Stella confronts the gesturally busy, spontaneous painting of Abstract Expressionism with entirely un-spontaneous, symmetrically organized compositions made up of stripes of the same shape. He emphasises the mechanical nature of the pictorial form and the genesis of the picture in the act of painting by using matt black house paint. This mechanical approach makes the expression and meaning of the painting seem extremely reduced—a polemical rejection of painting's claim to be art.

Symmetry and formal repetitiveness, the black paint less than perfectly applied and its impenetrable quality reinforce the impression of meaninglessness and apathy, which is further sustained by the title. Tomlinson Court Park is in a desolate suburb of New York. The other strip paintings in the series are named after disasters, coloured people's laments, or quote Nazi slogans. Demand's large-format photograph of a room shows a perfect reconstruction of the Führer's headquarters in the Wolfschanze after the attempt on Hitler's life. What we take to be a photographic reproduction of the pitch-black scene where the incident took place at night is nothing more than a picture of a paper reconstruction of the scene in minia-ture. Where we think we are seeing a real room, ultimately we are looking at a double illusion: a photographic image of a reconstructed underground place—the closely guarded secret hiding-place and command centre of evil that was remote from the rest of

the world and yet still terrorised it .
Which is closer to reality? A faithful
photographic reproduction of something that is unreal many times over,
or the non-representational picture?
HG

FRANK STELLA
∗ 1936 Malden

Tomlinson Court Park I, 1959
Enamel paint on canvas, 220 × 280 cm
Acquired 1973

THOMAS DEMAND
∗ 1964 Munich

Room, 1994
C-Print, diasec, 183 × 270 cm
Acquired 1996

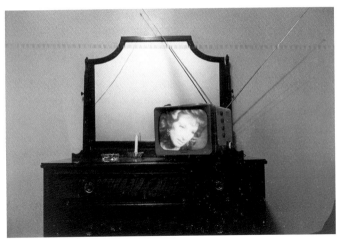

Portland, Maine, 1962: a dressing table with a mirror and a television set, its aerials reaching out into the room like feelers. The mirror shows emptiness, the candle in front of it is not lit. The face that the mirror normally reflects and the light the candle stands for are not here any more, but in the TV set—a perfect face in soot-free flickering.

The photographer of this memorable scene in which a mass medium ousts the everyday object by robbing it of its original function and significance made his name in America in the 1960s, working as Lee Friedlander. Reflections or shadows play an important part in many of his street scenes, monuments, self-portraits and series on the subject of work or unemployment. They mean that people or things are not viewed directly but are perceived only as reflections or images. They obey the principles of mediation and mediality, and express a typical state of mind in

LEE FRIEDLANDER
✳ 1934 Aberdeen

Portland, Maine, 1962
Gelatine silver, 19.2 × 28.5 cm
Acquired 1986

modern life in which reality can lose its concrete tangibility, but also gain a sense of poetry.

Gerhard Richter plays a similar game of emptying and simultaneous poeticisation by a process involving crossing media. He was born in East Germany in 1932 and moved to West Germany in 1961, and with Georg Baselitz and Sigmar Polke is one of Germany's major contemporary painters. Like Friedlander, Richter likes to work in series. The Cloud Picture (Wolkenbild) does not show a sky painted directly from nature, but just a reflection of it: Richter uses photographs that he translated into painting for his blurred images of realistic views. Thus the romantic sense of natural immediacy conveyed by this representation of an empty sky turns out to be the product of a highly developed technical process. *KyZ*

GERHARD RICHTER
∗ 1932 Waltersdorf

Cloud Picture no. 265, 1970
Oil on canvas, 220 × 300 cm
Acquired 1970

Photographs by Andreas Gursky, Sarah Jones and Philip Lorca di Corcia offer a critical, unsparing picture of the *conditio humana* in the last years of the 20th century. Gursky's **Bochum University** (Universität Bochum) gives us a view of the modern architecture of the educational reform project. The open hall supported by tall pillars has a chilly look, and has very few people in it. Only the creases on the couch in Sarah Jones's **Consulting Room (Couch)** tell us that a patient has just been lying there.

The impersonal and functional-looking space symbolises the conditions that constitute the psychic states of contemporary societies.

Philip Lorca di Corcia shows an equally anonymous non-place in **Alice**: solitary, harshly lit by flash, a middle-aged woman stands on a subway platform. The blurred lights of a train leaving the station can be seen in the background. The gesture her hands are making is met by emptiness: there is nothing for this woman to hold on to. *AM*

ANDREAS GURSKY
✳ 1955 Leipzig
Bochum University, 1988
C-Print, 44 × 60.5 cm
Acquired 1989

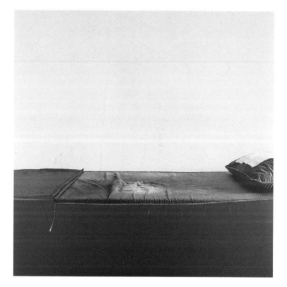

SARAH JONES
* 1959 London

Consulting Room (Couch) XXII, 1998
C-Print on aluminium, 152.4 × 152.4 cm
Acquired 2000

PHILIP LORCA DI CORCIA
* 1953 Hartford

Alice, 1988
C-Print, 41.9 × 58.2 cm
Acquired 1997

Crouching figures feature only infrequently in classical sculpture. They do not have the same symbolic and imposing force as standing or recumbent figures. Auguste Rodin deliberately broke away from academic tradition in the late 19ᵗʰ century, not just in his treatment of form but also in his choice of motifs. He chose individual forms or groups of figures—later also just fragments of human bodies—to represent people, sensations or emotions at individual and highly personal moments.

Crouching Woman (La Femme Accroupie) also seems to be more turned in on herself than to correspond to an ideal type of woman. Her body appears not in statuesque rigidity but captured at a fleeing moment. Her legs are wide apart and her torso is thrust forwards, revealing the intimacy of her womanhood. Rodin, who was also involved with the Symbolists, combines naturalistic detail with impressionist stylistic elements such as an emphasis on visual effects supporting the rich nuances of fleeting impressions. Even so, he also treats the figure as a mass to be kneaded and shaped. This produces an almost acrobatic interplay of limbs, coming together with supple fluidity and knotting themselves into axes twisted in different directions.

120 years later, Thomas Schütte achieved a similar result from precisely the opposite approach. At a time when sculptors had long since abandoned the

THOMAS SCHÜTTE
∗ 1954 Oldenburg
Steel Woman no. 11, 2002
Steel, 75 cm
Acquired 2002

human figure in order to make way for abstraction or installations, he recalled one of sculpture's very earliest forms, the female body. The first thing that strikes us about the figure of the **Steel Woman** (Stahlfrau), who is crouching over her knees, is the extreme elasticity of her limbs, also the way the torso and the lower part of the body are tightly clenched together and the backbone protudes through the tightly stretched skin. The quintessence of a smooth sporting body lacks the very thing that would make it into a human being— a head. Instead of this, a lip-like bulge thrusts forward, which could be read at best as an embryonic early form of a head. This is a being that seems strangely biomorphic and yet technoid, placed on an altar or dissecting table as if in an act of worship. *KyZ*

AUGUSTE RODIN
* 1842 Paris † 1917 Meudon
Crouching Woman, c. 1882
La Femme Accroupie
Bronze, 84 cm
Acquired by Karl Ernst Osthaus in 1903

Mark Rothko is one of the major exponents of American Colour Field painting after 1945, as can be seen from his rectangular patches of **white, pink and mustard** colour placed parallel to the frame and yet at the same time woolly in their indistinctness. They allow the colour to assert its intrinsic value with great intensity and at the same time elude our grasp. The harmoniously co-ordinated contrasts between the colour tones reinforce the impression of an inwardly pulsating pictorial space. The American artist Jessica Stockholder's **installation** translates Rothko's imaginary, inner-pictorial colour spaces into a constellation of colour fields and lines, in varying types of material within the confines of reality, ranging from the iridescent blue light of the lamps via the opaque yellow paint on the walls and the flecks of colour on the wooden laths to the colour of the carpet, itself only a background for coloured, geometrical

JESSICA STOCKHOLDER
* 1959 Seattle

Painting the Extended Field,
Room installation, 9 × 4.5 × 3 m
Acquired 2004

MARK ROTHKO
* 1903 Dvinsk/Daugavpils † 1970 New York

White, Pink and Mustard, 1954
Oil on canvas, 234 × 168.5 cm
Acquired 1978

shapes and coloured lines produced by ribbons, cords and woollen threads. Different manifestations of time emerge in this theatrical space. Switched-on standard lamps indicate the times of the day, revolving fans and threads moving in the draught make us aware that all existence is governed by time, while the fruit in the bowl indicates that things are transitory—and at the same time Stockholder forges a link with the tradition of still-life painting by juxtaposing fresh oranges, artificial bulbs and floral mattress covers. *HB*

The Folkwang Collections

EDOUARD MANET
* 1832 Paris † 1883 Paris

Singer Jean Baptiste Faure as Hamlet, 1877
Portrait de Chanteur Faure dans le Rôle
d'Hamlet
Oil on canvas, 194 × 131.5 cm
Acquired 1927

A museum of modernism.
The history of the painting collection

It took Ernst Gosebruch almost seven years to finish combining Osthaus's and the Essen art collections.

The Folkwang Museum opened its doors in the new building in Essen's Bismarckstrasse in 1929. Colleagues from other museums were impressed with the result. For example, Max Sauerlandt, director of the arts and crafts museum in Hamburg, wrote to Ernst Gosebruch on the occasion of his 60th birthday as follows: 'In the Folkwang you have placed sculptures and paintings by our immediate contemporaries quite simply right next to the highest and noblest masterpieces of past artistic epochs and from distant lands, … as though what was in dispute was the most natural thing in the world, to be completely taken for granted. By doing this, you have shown that something that could never be proved in theory is possible and effective: that the art of our day is not inferior to the art of the past, that the art of Asia and even of the "wild beasts" of European art, that the greatest creations of German art rank with the most noble works of French painting. You have thereby established a new type of contemporary museum in the purest sense.'

Gosebruch was not to enjoy his personal and highly valued triumph for long. Crude hostility from the political right wing, which came to a head following the sensational purchase of Manet's wonderful painting of singer Jean Baptiste Faure as Hamlet in 1927, proved a constant and debilitating sapping of morale. Ernst Gosebruch and the overwhelming majority of his museum colleagues, including the admiring Sauerlandt, were forced out of the museum service when the Nazis seized power in 1933 and had to watch from the sidelines as German museum history stood still for 12 years. One of the most drastic events in this period was undoubtedly the 'Degenerate Art' campaign that broke over the museums, not excepting the Folkwang, like a devastating fire in July and August 1937. Everything displeased the commission, which included Klaus, Count of Baudessin (appointed director of the Folkwang Museum), and/or was dated post-1910, was picked out in the first round and sent directly to Munich to appear in the exhibition of the same name. In a second sweep a little later, other works of art were sent to collection depots in Berlin. At this date, 1937, the politicians and the people involved in the campaign were not yet in agreement about what to do next.

An act passed in late May 1938 would change this. The museums affected had their artworks confiscated. Art by the Brücke and Blauer

Reiter groups and the Bauhaus—classic modernism henceforth no longer existed German museums. Covetous eyes from abroad for art that could be sold prompted the commission to look at the holdings again. Finally, even individual magnificent works by artists like the Norwegian Edvard Munch and particularly French paintings were taken from collections: Van Gogh's self-portrait from the Neue Pinakothek in Munich, his portrait of Dr. Gachet from the Von der Heydt Museum in Wuppertal, Paul Gauguin's *Marquisien à la Cape Rouge* from the Städelsches Kunstinstitut and Cézanne's Bibémus (ill. p. 73) from the Folkwang collection, which was then indisputably the home of modernism in Germany. The Folkwang lost other magnificent works, by artists including Georges Braque, Giorgio de Chirico, Edmund Cross, André Derain, but above all by Henri Matisse and Edvard Munch. It may sound like a miracle that the collection started by Karl Ernst Osthaus and vigorously continued by Ernst Gosebruch managed to keep major works by Paul Cézanne, Paul Gauguin, Vincent van Gogh, Paul Signac and one picture by Matisse, the still life Asphodel (ill p. 99). These are now among the Folkwang's outstanding treasures.

Ernst Gosebruch was not just a friend of Hagen collector and benefactor Karl Ernst Osthaus, but was committed like his friend to promoting progressive currents in art. Gosebruch was responsible for building up the Essen art collections from 1906, and was appointed director of the young Essen institution in 1909. It was no coincidence that he followed the same line as Osthaus, acquiring French works, German Expressionists, but also Romantic pictures—of course, all within the financial framework laid down for him by the coalmining and industrial town of Essen. So it was a most fulfilling moment for him when the administrator of Osthaus's estate wrote to the Essen art institute in 1922 proposing that it buy the Hagen collection. By then Gosebruch was very familiar with Essen's business world, and so he knew how to come up with the necessary funds. The purchasers founded the Folkwang Museum Association, which then as now guaranteed the continuity of this art institution, together with the local authority.

The first priority for building up the collections in Hagen and Essen was always personal contact with artists and an unswerving commitment to contemporary art. Osthaus's institutional and financial independence meant that he could implement his ideas and plans for his new museum immediately. Another of his fundamental principles was that he bought works for his collection directly from the artists. The young collector did not have the pleasure of meeting Van Gogh and Gauguin. The visit to Cézanne by Osthaus and his wife in April

PIERRE AUGUSTE RENOIR
∗ 1841 Limoges † 1919 Cagnes

Olive Grove, c. 1910
Oil on canvas, 32 × 48 cm
Acquired by Karl Ernst Osthaus in 1912

Still Life with Apples, c. 1910
Nature Morte aux Pommes
Oil on canvas, 21.5 × 23.5 cm
Acquired by Karl Ernst Osthaus in 1912

Portrait of Gertrud Osthaus, 1913
Portrait de Gertrud Osthaus
Oil on canvas, 55 × 46.5 cm
Acquired by Karl Ernst Osthaus in 1913

was inspired not just by the idea of paying his respects to the venerable old master, but also by the intention of acquiring works for Hagen. The great Frenchman agreed to make a list of his works available to the German for selection. That this did not happen was certainly because the artist died in October the same year (1906). The two Cézanne pictures remaining in the Folkwang, Maison de Bellevue and Dovecote and Quarry at Bibémus (ill. pp. 72, 73) Osthaus bought from the painter's Paris dealer Ambroise Vollard in 1906/07.

Personal contact with Auguste Renoir was not made until a good ten years later, after the spectacular acquisition of Lise (ill. p. 61), painted in 1867, in 1901. In 1912/13, three more works came into the Hagen collection, an Olive Grove, a Still Life with Apples and the Portrait of Gertrud Osthaus. These works were purchased on a visit to the master in Cagnes in the South of France and — with the greatest respect — should be seen more as a gracious acknowledgement, a memento of a wonderful meeting between the collector and his wife and Renoir.

Apart from local artists and Christian Rohlfs, who moved to Hagen from Weimar in 1901, Osthaus seems to have made his first regular contact with an artist in the person of Auguste Rodin. Osthaus visited Rodin's studio several times from 1901 onwards. The four life-size sculptures purchased by 1904, Faun and Nymph, The Bronze Age, Eve and Crouching Woman, confirm the soundness of his interest in Rodin (ills. pp. 43, 64, 66, 203), aimed at giving 'the five million people in our industrial area the opportunity to admire the lofty spirit and the exquisite beauty of your art.'

At the time the museum was founded, Karl Ernst Osthaus had started to take an interest in French and Belgian artists—not least because his adviser Henry van de Velde knew so much about them. There are therefore considerable numbers of works by Belgians George Minne, Theo van Rysselberghe and Constantin Meunier in the Hagen collection. Paintings like Madonna and Child (The Kiss) by Maurice Denis were among the first works by the artist ever to find their way into a German public collection. It is possible that Osthaus decided to buy the work because he was persuaded to by Harry, Graf (Count) Kessler, the diplomat, aesthete and director of the Weimar art collections. Graf Kessler admired Denis, and showed seven loans from him in Weimar in 1903.

Paul Signac's 1900 painting of the Seine at St. Cloud (ill. p.103) was also the first work by the neo-Impressionist to find its way into a German museum. It is possible that this work too had been shown in Weimar by Graf Kessler, and been acquired there or via appropriate contacts by Osthaus. Hence this painting by Signac and the Denis work were in Hagen before 1905. Years later, shortly before the outbreak of the First World War, Ernst Gosebruch managed to acquire two works by the Pointillist virtuoso for the Essen collection from the Paris dealer Bernheim-Jeune. These were Paris, Île de la Cité and The Pink Tower, Marseilles, dating from 1912 and 1913 respectively.

Osthaus also once owned two works by Georges Seurat, the father of all Pointillists, but he soon sold them again—with hindsight, a regrettable decision by the collector.

Osthaus had particularly close ties with Christian Rohlfs. It was certainly Henry van de Velde's unerring instincts and Osthaus's foresight that led them to promote this artist, who had lived and worked in Weimar for almost 30 years, and set up the framework that had led to his ultra-rapid development as an artist in subsequent years. After a short stay in Berlin, Rohlfs had studied, with very few interruptions, at the grand ducal art academy in Weimar founded in 1860, which was progressive by reputation. He then made the town of Goethe and Schiller, Herder and Nietzsche the focal point in his life, amidst a richly cultural landscape that was still remote from the industrialisation and politicisation of the new society developing in the early 20th century. In 1902, Rohlfs took an apartment and studio on the first floor of the newly opened Folkwang museum building. Osthaus brought other young artists to Hagen as well as Rohlfs, in the conviction that they would support his idea of realising a flourishing cultural scene: these included the much younger painter and graphic artist Emil

Rudolf Weiss from Karlsruhe, Jan Thorn-Prikker, who specialized in stained glass, sculptress Milly Steeger, and Moissey Kogan from Russia. Sculptor Willy Lammert and painter Walter Bötticher, both from Hagen, joined the Folkwang artists' circle later, as did Dutch applied artist J. L. Mathieu Lauweriks. Osthaus successfully engaged well-known architects like Peter Behrens and Richard Riemerschmidt for ambitious urban development projects in Hagen. They all benefited from the (for the time unusually upbeat) mood of change in the industrial town.

The Folkwang Museum in Hagen became increasingly significant culturally, and artists also became ever more interested in the art institution, which was able to develop independently of the prevailing Wilhelminian political dogma. Osthaus began to invite artists to Hagen to make small-scale presentations. This turned out to be an effective device for studying exhibits in detail and considering them for purchase. Works like Ferdinand Hodler's Spring (ill. p. 97) found a new home in the collection in this way. Other items in the collection are reminders of exhibitions of George Minne, Constantin Meunier, Wilhelm Trübner, Vincent van Gogh, Edvard Munch, Emil Bernard, Oskar Kokoschka, Alexander Archipenko and many others. The Matisse exhibition in December 1907 is also immortalised in the Folkwang collection. The collector had acquired the Asphodel (ill. p. 99) in Paris in the previous October. This was followed in 1909 by the River Landscape (now in the Kunstmuseum in Basle) and Bathers with Turtles (now in the St. Louis Art Museum), and by the end of 1913 Osthaus had bought a fourth painting by Matisse, the Blue Windows (now in the Museum of Modern Art), years after Matisse, accompanied by Hans Purrmann and Henry van de Velde, had visited the collector and his museum on his way back from Berlin to Paris in December 1908.

Particularly the artists from the Brücke group of artists in Dresden and the Neue Künstlervereinigung in Munich, from which the Blauer Reiter seceded, made contact with the private museum in Hagen at a very early stage. The correspondence started late in 1906. The first presentation by the Dresden artists was in June 1906, and in June 1910 came another group exhibition by the 'Junge Wilden'. As well as this, Osthaus worked vigorously on behalf of Emil Nolde, putting him, like the Brücke artists, in touch with comprehensive exhibitions by the Sonderbund Westdeutscher Künstler, whose committees Osthaus regularly served on. From about 1912 Ernst Ludwig Kirchner would enter into an ever more lively correspondence with Osthaus. These letters record projects for Kirchner's participation in the Cologne Werkbund exhibition in 1914, the intensive exchange of ideas, and his involvement in painting the dome of the City Hall in Hagen and the competition for the Iron Smith of Hagen.

The artists from the Neue Künstlervereinigung München and the Blauer Reiter that emerged from it, Vassily Kandinsky, August Macke, Franz Marc and Gabriele Münter, were in touch with the Hagen Folkwang Museum and showed their work in four group exhibitions in various combinations. August Macke had already been to Hagen for the first time in 1908, and reported to Bernhard Koehler, his fiancée's uncle, in Berlin: 'It is an exceptionally beautiful collection, of the kind that probably seldom comes together. It not only has the best modernists but old things as well, a lot of Egyptian, Greek, Indian, Gothic and Italian. We were quite infatuated (*jeck*), as they say here.'

The parallels between the Essen art collection directed by Ernst Gosebruch and the Hagen Folkwang are obvious. Gosebruch championed Emil Nolde, supported the Sonderbund and exhibition tours by the various artists' groups and vigorously pursued contacts with contemporary artists. Gosebruch had been friendly with Essen-born chemist Carl Hagemann since 1910, and had helped him to build up his own collection over the decades. In turn, Hagemann offered him considerable support in setting up an institute of contemporary art. Gosebruch asked Willi Baumeister, Erich Heckel, Ludwig Gies, Oskar Schlemmer and Ernst Ludwig Kirchner to prepare designs for the new museum galleries in which the Essen and Hagen collections were to be brought together in 1929. Political and human setbacks stood in the way of realising these magnificent plans. Finally the Nazis wantonly sabotaged the joint development of the two perfectly matched collections that Gosebruch—working entirely in the spirit of Karl Ernst Osthaus—had expanded consistently until he was forced to resign in October 1933.

The new beginning came in 1945. Heinz Köhn, who had been the circumspect director of the Essen Folkwang Museum since 1938, and his young assistant Paul Vogt had not only lost all the works of classic modernism produced after 1910 and/or that displeased the fanatical Nazis but the building itself had been destroyed in an air raid. Nevertheless, in 1960 the first new museum building in the new Federal Republic opened on its historical site. Subsequently Paul Vogt, director of the Essen Folkwang from 1963 to 1988, managed to replace the lost holdings, above all among the classic modernists, with works of exceptional quality, and also to secure important examples of later styles such as Informel, New Figuration and American Abstract Expressionism for the collection.

The museum inherited the 19th century collection and the lavish collection of international applied art and items from antiquity. The

ALBERT RENGER PATZSCH
Rotunda, Folkwang Museum, Essen, 1931
George Minne: Fountain with Boys,
Oskar Schlemmer: Wall paintings

presentation of all sections of the collection, together with examples from the Graphic Art and Photographic collections, meant that the distinction of the pre-war period could be matched. But over and above this, the extensive new holdings made it uniquely possible to present 19th and 20th century painting and art items that are traditionally housed in separate museums together, in a community of free and applied art.

Mario-A. von Lüttichau
KEEPER, PAINTING AND SCULPTURE COLLECTION

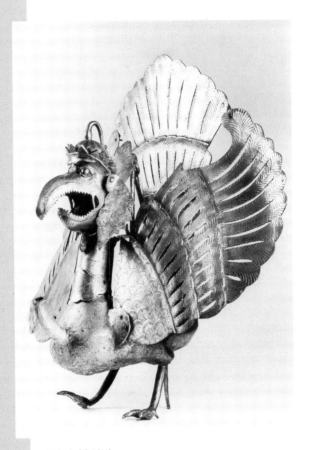

INDIA OR JAVA
**Garuda bird, lamp for a *wayang kulit* play,
18/19C**
Brass, 57 cm
Acquired 1931

Art in dialogue.
The applied art department

The modern painting collection is not the Folkwang Museum's only claim to distinction. The great applied art collection hones the eye for striking parallels between fine and applied art. If one relaxes into the association game, it is possible to understand what may have prompted Karl Ernst Osthaus to underline such connections with his extensive art collection. His activities as a collector included applied and small art items from the outset. His enthusiasm for exhibits from the Middle East must have been fired by his visit to Tunis in 1897. The first purchases may date from this time. Subsequently, craft objects were obtained from all periods from Germany, Europe and non-European countries so as to provide new ideas for contemporary art, but also to inspire also local industry by providing top quality models that set standards for silversmiths and firms working with textiles and ceramics to follow. The selection in the museum's departments was more like a model didactic collection than items of ethnographical or art-historical interest. This collecting method of Karl Ernst Osthaus's and the practical work of the Folkwang Museum led in 1909 to the epoch-making concept of the German Museum of Art in Trade and Industry, instituted by the Deutscher Werkbund. The aim of this Hagen-based institute was to compile a model collection of high-quality craft exhibits and create an art-educational centre, though unfortunately it never had a building of its own. Exhibitions of items in the museum's collection therefore took place in Hagen, Krefeld and Düsseldorf.

The Folkwang Museum's applied arts collection now includes exhibits from Africa, Central America, Asia, the South Seas and of course Europe, also antiquities from Greece and Egypt, Iraq and Iran, and extensive collections of tiles, textiles and glass from ancient times to the modern era. The directors of the Folkwang Museum after Karl Ernst Osthaus also felt committed to building up this department, as can be seen from two exhibits, the garuda bird from Java (acquired by Ernst Gosebruch) and the Chinese Kuei bronze (acquired by Paul Vogt).

Exhibits from all continents and a variety of epochs give the collection its extraordinary character. The museum has Emil Nolde's friendship with Karl Ernst Osthaus to thank for the magnificent works in its South Seas collection. Nolde, who had accompanied an Imperial Colonial Office medical-demographic expedition to German New

Guinea in 1913, met the Hagen-born New Guinean German Franz Wiesener at this time, who presented his collection to the museum in 1915. It included Uli and Malanggan figures, ceremonial shields and ancestor boards, the ridge beams of a men's house and some everyday utensils.

Alongside the South Seas exhibits, African art provides a second focal point. In 1914, the Museum and Ethnographic Institute in Hamburg offered Karl Ernst Osthaus the chance to acquire items from the Leo Frobenius Collection, which the explorer of Africa had collected as part of the German African Interior Exploration Expedition in 1910. These exhibits were shown at the Hagen Folkwang in July 1914, one of the first exhibitions of African art in Germany.

The American continent is represented in the Folkwang by Mexican stone sculptures and a multi-faceted Peruvian ceramics collection from the sites in Moche and Nasca.

The large tile collection was essentially assembled in the years 1908 and 1909. It was among other people Walter Gropius, the founder of the Bauhaus, who made purchases for Osthaus in Spain. In 1911 Osthaus published an essay on the format of tiles, the qualities of their clay, cobalt and lustre painting, the handling of colour glazes and the various local types. He was the first academic to research this topic. 'The various techniques for individual lead glazes are discussed, then faïence mosaic and the process for fixing different glazes on the same surface, the colour scales of different locations are explored and the distribution areas investigated.' In the context of these acquisitions, mention must be made of the Islamic-style lustre ceramics from Spain in the collection, and one of the rare large Alhambra wing vases.

In the first decade of the 20th century, Karl Ernst Osthaus was able to acquire outstanding Egyptian art exhibits, prehistoric stone vases and pre-dynastic ceramics, and also small sculptures in limestone, bronze and wood dating back to the Hellenic period. Another key area is Greek ceramics: geometrical, Corinthian and Attic vessels, and a selection of Tanagra figures. Roman antiquity is represented by Etruscan vases and a large number of glasses. This department of classical antiquity in particular grew considerably under Paul Vogt.

Karl Ernst Osthaus was also aware of the influence of Far Eastern art on European art at an early stage. The Folkwang collections still have large holdings of Chinese, Japanese and Korean ceramics. The Korean and Japanese ceramics relate largely to the tea ceremony. The Asian collection is completed with tea caddies and drinking bowls that cannot be dated beyond the 18th century, but come from famous old

CHINA
Kuei bronze, Chou Dynasty, 9C BC
Bronze, 16.3 cm
Acquired 1962

FLEMISH?
Eagle lectern, 14C
Wrought iron, gilt, 75 cm
[Karl Ernst Osthaus Collection]

potteries like Seto and Bizen, along with Oribe or Raku ware, lacquer work such as *suzuribako* (writing boxes), *inro* and *netsuke* (multipartite containers and their fastenings), wrought Tsuba work (sword guards), and sculptures from China, Japan, Thailand, India and Burma. An exceptional feature of great interest from Asia is a collection of Javanese *wayang kulit* figures acquired in Amsterdam around 1909 together with a large number of Japanese Nô and Kyogen masks, which Osthaus acquired from the estate of Swiss painter Benjamin Vautier, who died in Düsseldorf in 1898.

The collection of sample textiles deserves special mention. It includes over 200 exhibits, including 60 Coptic textiles alone. Ecclesiastical vestments mingle with Asian garments, Javanese batik goods with rococo fabrics—in short, it was a collection intended for careful study by the local textile industry, as a source of new ideas for designers.

Figures of saints, bronze crucifixes and bronze utensils take us to the Romanesque and Gothic periods, such as the eagle lectern from Flanders. Finally the collection of Art Nouveau vases (Gallé, Daum and Tiffany) should be mentioned, as one of the last large gifts to the applied arts department. It was presented to the collection in 1956.

Ulrike Köcke
HEAD OF THE MUSEUM EDUCATION SERVICE
KEEPER, APPLIED ARTS COLLECTION

PAUL KLEE
∗ 1879 Münchenbuchsee † 1940 Muralto

Sunken Landscape, 1918, 65
Landscape with Sky Flower
Watercolour, gouache and pen on paper,
glossy paper strips added top and bottom,
on card, 17.6 × 16.3 cm
Acquired 1958

The history of the Graphic Art Collection

Much has been written, and in great detail, about his treasures since Karl Ernst Osthaus founded the Folkwang Museum in Hagen in 1902. Here attention is particularly directed towards the classic modernist works that undoubtedly are still the key feature of the collection. But people tend to forget that the museum also has a not insubstantial collection of works from the late 18th and 19th centuries. There is far too little awareness of the astonishing range of styles and approaches in this period, which is at least as varied as the 20th century. Here I will mention only the main areas covered in the museum's holdings.

Chronologically speaking, we start with the artists who make use of Baroque forms to establish art for the well-to-citizen. These include Daniel Nikolaus Chodwiecki and Jean Baptiste Greuze. Then come the Romantics with their main exponent Caspar David Friedrich and the Nazarene group, characterized by their spare drawing method, approaching the classical style in its formal austerity. Even though artists such as Peter Cornelius, Friedrich Johann Overbeck and Julius Schnorr von Carolsfeld saw monumental fresco art as their supreme task, their drawings are particularly effective in sharpening and singling out what they saw. Joseph Anton Koch's heroic landscapes and mythical themes represent the neoclassical approach. After the Romantics, realistic themes appear, in terms of both landscapes and also figures, as in the work of Adolf Menzel and Franz Krüger. As well as this, it is possible to see a strong inclination towards illustration and literary exposition.

At this point works by Ludwig Richter, Moritz von Schwind and Carl Spitzweg come to the fore, asserting that small, close at hand domestic items were worthy of depiction. They take us into the quiet world of everyday life, humorously, ironically and in the spirit of fairy-tales. Other artists again, hostile to poetry, were more inclined towards theory, after the publication of Adolf von Hildebrand's *The Problem of Form in Fine Art*; these include Hans von Marées.

In general, one may say of 19th century graphics in the Folkwang Museum that the collection is especially sound on the first half of the century. Here it should be remembered that Marburg theology professor Karl Budde left the Essener Kunstmuseum an extensive and important Ludwig Richter collection as early as 1906, and this formed a focal point for further acquisitions. The artists collected were those that obviously expanded this basic holding. The same policy was pursued when the Kunstmuseum merged with the Hagen Folkwang Museum in

ADRIAN LUDWIG RICHTER
✳ 1803 Dresden † 1884 Loschwitz
Children Playing, 1848
Pen and watercolour, 11.9 × 20.9 cm
Acquired 1907

1922. Under the Third Reich in particular, when modernist artists were being rubbished, collecting proceeded in this direction. Works by Caspar David Friedrich, Wilhelm von Kobell, Franz Krüger and Alfred Rethel came into the museum at this time.

When the Hagen Folkwang moved to Essen, the graphic art collection grew considerably under the new director Ernst Gosebruch. He was particularly receptive to contemporary art, and moved into a new field by acquiring German Expressionist drawings and printed graphics, with Emil Nolde and Ludwig Kirchner particularly well represented. The entire 19th and 20th century graphic art collection was presented in concentrated form for the first time in a catalogue published in 1929. The Third Reich's cultural policies put an abrupt stop to further expansion of the collection, which by then was of international significance. About 1200 items were confiscated in the 1937 'Degenerate Art' campaign and disappeared forever. Almost all the holdings of watercolours, drawings and printed graphics acquired after 1900 were lost at this point. It was a happy chance that a very few drawings by Pablo Picasso and Henri Matisse remained in the museum. Lists made at the time were incomplete, so give only a hint of the true loss.

Money was short in the post-war years, so mainly printed graphic art was collected. Here the 20th century was again to the fore, appropriately to the house tradition. It was particularly important to fill in the gaps in the German Expressionist section, which is still a key feature of the collection as a whole. A considerable step forward came in 1957, not only with the acquisition of all Christian Rohlfs's printed graphics, but also with a large number of his drawings and watercolours. In the same way, the almost complete printed graphic work of Erich Heckel was acquired in the sixties, including hand prints, some of which are valuable. Of course it was in the museum's interest not to neglect art after 1945, tending mainly towards abstract works, and contemporary art is still being added to the Graphic Art Collection at the time of writing.

The works illustrated in this guide in the context of other works can only give a hint of the abundance of graphic art available, and they are intended to whet the appetite for seeing the originals.

Hubertus Froning
KEEPER, GRAPHIC ART COLLECTION

SAM FRANCIS
* 1923 San Mateo † 1994 Venice, LA
Composition, 1960
Gouache on paper, 21.3 × 35.4 cm
Acquired 1961

View of the slide display in the Steinert
Study Room

The history of the Photographic Collection

The Photographic Collection in the Folkwang Museum has been in existence for a little over 25 years, but the Folkwang name has been linked with the appreciation of and commitment to photography as a pictorial device for much longer: Karl Ernst Osthaus, who opened the Folkwang Museum in Hagen in 1902, mounted an international exhibition of professional photography as early as 1903, and included pictures by Hugo Erfurth, Rudolf Dührkoop, Nicola Perscheid and Jacob Hilfsdorf in an applied art exhibition organised for the USA in 1912.

The latest trends in photography in the twenties were presented in Essen after the First World War under the influence of Kurt Wilhelm-Kästner, who worked at the Folkwang Museum from 1923 to 1933. He initiated the 'Contemporary Photography' project in 1929, even before the legendary Werkbund 'Film and Photography' exhibition. Then came an exhibition called 'Das Lichtbild' (The Photograph) and in 1933 the first solo show for French photographer and Bauhaus student Florence Henri.

Two other names are important when we look back over the photographic tradition in Essen. Albert Renger-Patzsch had his studio in the Folkwang Museum from 1929 to 1944, the year when the building was destroyed. The extensive section of his work dealing with the Ruhr dates from this period.

And after the Second World War, Werner Graeff and Max Burchartz, who had been re-engaged for the foundation course, made efforts to pick up the threads established in the twenties. Otto Steinert, who took over the Folkwangschule photography class, was able to make contact with Albert Renger-Patzsch and Max Burchartz again in the early sixties, and acquired a number of their works.

Steinert was able to put on an exhibition of the Gernsheim Collection in the Folkwang Museum in his first year in Essen, 1959. Thus his activities as a visiting curator started with the first of the annual 'Contributions to the history of photography' series of exhibitions, which continued until his death in 1978. He had made contact with the Folkwang immediately after being appointed to Essen, and suggested setting up a collection on the history of photography.

Astonishingly, Steinert succeeded as early as 1961 in persuading the city of Essen's art politicians to accept his plan; showing the Gernsheim Collection had been a shrewd move in softening them up for this. He managed to buy the crucial nucleus for a future civic collection at the photography auction in Geneva in the same year—including 144 calotypes by the Scottish portrait artists David Octavius Hill and Robert Adamson alone, and also a choice selection of 19th century architectural photographs.

Various groups of works were added to the collection in the course of Steinert's almost 20 years of teaching in Essen. Paul Vogt, who was director of the Folkwang Museum at the time, supported the annual exhibition projects and purchase contacts. It was thanks to him that in 1978, after Steinert's death, this study collection was not only taken over by the Folkwang Museum, but also formed the basis for the foundation of an independent department.

Even though the Folkwangschule für Gestaltung had become part of the Essen Gesamthochschule in 1972, meaning that North Rhine-Westphalia was now responsible for it, the photographic collection, which had been built up with municipal funds, was still available to the school for its teaching.

When the 'Photographic Collection at the Folkwang Museum' department was set up in autumn 1978, the element of photographic training initiated by Steinert, unique in Germany at the time, of teaching the history of photography using original examples came to an end. But the collection remained in Essen, and has been open to the public since then.

The collection and the department were crucially expanded thanks to the personal commitment of Paul Vogt and his contacts with regional foundations. The main thrust of the work lay in opening up the archived holdings and processing them academically; the results appeared regularly in publications. In subsequent years, both the private picture collection and the library, and later Steinert's photographic estate, were secured for the Folkwang Museum, and an important set of works relating to August Sander and twenties portrait photography were acquired with the aid of the Alfried Krupp von Bohlen und Halbach Foundation.

Given the photographic activities in Essen described here, founding a Photographic Collection at the Folkwang Museum seemed a logical and natural next step, which raises the question of why there was a delay. During the Folkwangschule teacher's period as a visiting curator, Paul Vogt had repeatedly tried to persuade Steinert to make his collection part of the Folkwang Museum. At the time, neither insurance values nor conservation-related arguments presented key argument for housing the collection in the museum, so Steinert apparently had no reason to refuse non-bureaucratic access to the holdings at any time, and anyway he tended to treat it as his private property when

View of the Helen Chadwick 'Essluna' exhibition, 1994

View of the Patrick Toskani exhibition, 1997

dealing with researchers' enquiries. But his commitment and success in building up the collection he started in 1959, its use in his teaching and the exhibitions he organised in parallel with the Folkwang Museum did much for photographic education and interest in photographic history in Germany.

From 1978 to 1983, until the museum's new building was completed, the collection remained on the Folkwangschule premises. The holdings were catalogued in this period, which was also used for purchasing a series of estates and collections.

The Photographic Collection's work concentrates on five key areas: conserving the holdings, a temporary exhibition programme, continuous new acquisitions, processing the collection academically and ensuring public access to it. The annual exhibition programme includes about six projects, working towards alternating historical and contemporary exhibitions, or creating links between the two.

We see presenting contemporary ways of using photography and its historical modes of depiction or alternating thematic group exhibitions and isolated oeuvre retrospectives as a meaningful way of getting across photographic pictorial achievements and the forms they took.

In 1982, the Folkwang Museum made a forward-looking move in terms of contemporary photography that was very well received in Germany, with the assistance of the Alfried Krupp von Bohlen und Halbach Foundation and the personal commitment of Berthold Beitz. The Foundation has used the scholarships that have been awarded since then to initiate a discussion that has attracted other prizes and support. Then, in the year 2000, a funding programme was launched, in co-operation with the Foundation, for up-and-coming photography curators. This is carried out in co-operation with the Kupferstichkabinett in Dresden and the Photographic Museum in Munich. The Dietrich Oppenberg Foundation is to be thanked for initiating the Albert Renger Patzsch Prize. This is a European photographic book prize that has been awarded for a book production every three years since 1991.

Another key funding aspect relates to the Photographic Collection's outside activities. Young art and photography historians are given the opportunity to devise and run courses, guided tours and workshop discussions as part of the exhibition programme.

The collection's principal periods covered are the 1920s, the 1950s and the present day. But the 19th century is also represented by some outstanding creative work, especially in the collection's main thematic areas: depicting people and architecture, or the built environment.

The treatment of photography in museums was and remains a challenge, as a large proportion of photographic practice came into being for a specific purpose. Increasing contemporary interest in photographic exhibitions will probably lead to changes in museum work. The urgent aims in the field of photographic history lie in compiling surveys of work, and researching particular periods, themes and areas in which photography is used. Particular attention should be paid to changed forms of perception relating to historical development and the way photographs are responded to in this context. The introduction of new media presents the museum with new fields for its work. But dealing with them makes it clear that photography is in a long tradition of creative processes and is the 20th century's most important means of communication. It is not possible to understand current media developments without a knowledge of photographic pictorial propositions.

Ute Eskildsen
HEAD OF THE PHOTOGRAPHIC COLLECTION

HENRI DE TOULOUSE-LAUTREC
* 1864 Albi † 1901 Gironde

Le Matin, **1893**
Colour lithograph, 83 × 59.5 cm

The history of the German Poster Museum in Essen

The success of the *Posters by French Masters around 1900* exhibition of posters bought by the Folkwangschule shortly before prepared the ground for the founding of the Deutsches Plakat Museum e.V. in 1969. The association's aim was to set up a German Poster Museum based in Essen, and was able to present the first exhibition in its own name in 1970. When the Folkwangschule was subsumed into the newly founded university known as the Gesamthochschule Essen in 1973, the newly responsible authorities wished to dispense with the poster collection and it went over to the municipal authorities in Essen a year later.

The Deutsches Plakat Museum was attached to the Folkwang Museum in organisational terms and until 2001 run by Frieder Mellinghoff. The museum first established a permanent presence in the Haus Industrieform / Old Synagogue. In the early eighties the Deutsches Plakat Museum moved into premises in Rathenaustrasse, also in the centre. At first this could be used only for storage purposes.

The exhibition galleries were not opened in the same complex until 1983, when the much-admired exhibitions were at last on show in a building of their own. This meant that the museum was able to establish a good reputation in Germany and beyond. Numerous exhibitions and competitions were held, and the collection was also rapidly and actively expanded. But there seemed to be no scope for devoting appropriate attention to the collection itself as the basis of the museum. In the long term, this led to a neglect of both systematic collecting and the possibility of focused research on the basis of the collection.

As the collection grew over the years, another move had to be contemplated. In 2004 the foundations were laid for a fresh start. The first step was to move the collection to premises that were future-proof and appropriate in terms of conservation. Such a place was found in the Zukunft Zentrums Zollverein (Triple Z), where over 280,000 posters found a new home. The collection is now adequately housed and its future secure. Formal and academic classification of the collection has been taking place in various phases since 2005. Creating a sound academic archive of the collection is now central to the activities, alongside restoration and conservation. A database has been set up to assess and process the items.

JAN TSCHICHOLD
✶ 1902 Leipzig   † 1974 Berzona
Piquedame / with Jenny Jugo and Rud. Forster, 1928
Letterpress printing, 119 × 84 cm

The intention is that the museum should reopen in 2006. The new location will then be the Zeche Zollverein.

The Deutsches Plakat Museum documents the development of the German poster in a European context. It is not aiming at completeness, but at being able to track developments and mutual influences within European poster development as a whole, with a number of typical non-European examples alongside for comparison.

The collection contains over 340,000 posters overall, from the fields of politics, economics and culture. In terms of time, it runs from the early days of poster development to the present day. The collection includes pieces by well-known artists and innovative designs, and also posters as documents of day-to-day history. Collecting activity focuses on the late 19th and 20th centuries. Thematic divisions are early German posters, First World War posters, Weimar Republic posters, post-war posters, posters from East and West Germany up to 1990 and Federal Republic posters from 1990. As well as this, the Deutsches Plakat Museum is also interested in international poster art in various special collections, for example French, Polish and Swiss posters.

This extensive and internationally directed collection is made

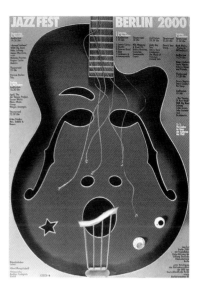

RICHARD BLANK
* 1901 Berlin † 1972 West Berlin
Ssh! / The Enemy's Listening, 1943/44
Offset, 58.2 × 42 cm

GÜNTHER KIESER
* 1930 Kronberg (Taunus)
Jazz Festival, Berlin 2000, 2000
Offset, 119 × 84 cm

possible by generous donations from private collectors, public and private institutions, numerous companies and businesses from the Essen area and not least the Deutsches Plakat-Forum e.V.

René Grohnert
HEAD OF THE DEUTSCHES PLAKAT MUSEUM

Catalogues of the collections at the Folkwang Museum, Essen

Museum Folkwang Hagen. Moderne Kunst. Vol. I. Hagen, 1912

Museum Folkwang Hagen. Moderne Kunst. Vol. I. Essen, 1929

Führer durch das Museum Folkwang Essen. Recklinghausen, 1964

Museum Folkwang Essen. Handzeichnungen des 19. Jahrhunderts. Essen, 1966

Museum Folkwang Essen. Katalog der Sammlung javanischer Schatten-spielfiguren. Essen, undated

Museum Folkwang Essen. Katalog der Gemälde des 19. und 20. Jahrhunderts. Essen, 1969.

From the museum's collections. Essen: Haus Industrieform, Essen: Deutsches Plakat Museum, 1970

Museum Folkwang Essen. Katalog der Gemälde des 19. Jahrhunderts. Essen, 1971

Museum Folkwang Essen. Katalog der Gemälde des 20. Jahrhunderts. Essen, 1971

1. Triennale. Essen: Deutsches Plakat Museum, 1972

Museum Folkwang Essen. Katalog der Bildwerke. Essen: Museum Folkwang, 1973

Museum Folkwang Essen. Katalog der Gemälde des 19. Jahrhunderts. Essen: Museum Folkwang, 1981

Museum Folkwang Essen. Katalog der Gemälde des 20. Jahrhunderts. Essen: Museum Folkwang, 1981

Museum Folkwang Essen. Katalog der griechischen und italienischen Vasen. Essen: Museum Folkwang, 1982

Helmar Lerski. Lichtbildner. Fotografien und Filme 1910–1947. Essen: Museum Folkwang, 1982

Helmar Lerski. Verwandlungen durch Licht. Essen: Museum Folkwang, 1982

Paul Vogt, Museum Folkwang Essen: Die Geschichte einer Sammlung junger Kunst im Ruhrgebiet. Cologne: DuMont, 1983

Japanische Plakate—Aus Tradition in Gegenwart und Zukunft. Essen: Deutsches Plakat Museum, 1984

Die Afrika-Sammlungen der Essener Museen. Essen: Museum Folkwang, 1985

Sammlung Otto Steinert. Reprint. Essen: Museum Folkwang, 1985

5. Triennale: Die besten Plakate der Jahre 1984 bis 1986. Essen: Deutsches Plakat Museum, 1987

Georg W. Költzsch: Bilder für eine Sammlung: Museum Folkwang Essen. Essen/Cologne: Museum Folkwang/ DuMont, 1994

ringl + pit. Ellen Auerbach und Grete Stern. Essen: Museum Folkwang, 1993

László Moholy-Nagy. Fotogramme 1922–1943. Essen: Museum Folkwang, 1995

Lotte Errell, Reporterin der 30er Jahre. Essen: Museum Folkwang, 1997

Kindheit ist kein Kinderspiel (Internat. poster competition). Essen: Deutsches Plakat Museum, 1998

Verfahren der Fotografie. Expanded edition. Essen: Museum Folkwang, 1999

Der Fotograf Otto Steinert. Essen: Museum Folkwang, 1999

Germaine Krull. Avantgarde als Abenteuer. Leben und Werk der Fotografin. Essen: Museum Folkwang, 1999

'Wenn Berlin Biarritz wäre…' Architektur in Bildern der Fotografischen Sammlung im Museum Folkwang. Essen, 2001

Georg W. Költzsch: Phoenix Folkwang. Die Meisterwerke. Essen: Museum Folkwang, 2002

Helmar Lerski. Verwandlungen durch Licht. Aus dem Bestand des Museum Folkwang. Essen: Museum Folkwang, 2002

Erwerbungen seit 1995—Gefördert durch die Stiftung Presse-Haus NRZ. Aus dem Bestand des Museum Folkwang. Essen: Museum Folkwang, 2002

Kinder sind der Rhythmus dieser Welt. Essen: Deutsches Plakat Museum, 2002

Ein Bilderbuch. Die fotografische Sammlung im Museum Folkwang. Essen: Museum Folkwang, 2003

'Was ich von ihnen gesehen und was man mir von ihnen erzählt hatte.' Der fotografierte Mensch in Bildern der Fotografischen Sammlung im Museum Folkwang. Essen: Museum Folkwang, 2003

Folkwang. Erstes Museum der Moderne, Gauguin, Van Gogh bis Dalí. Munich: Kunsthalle der Hypo-Kulturstiftung, 2004

Aquarelle und Zeichnungen des 19. Jahrhunderts im Museum Folkwang Essen. Essen: Museum Folkwang, 2005

Ferdinand Hodler, Der Frühling, Kunstwerkefolkwang 01, Essen 2005

Imprint

Published by Museum Folkwang, Essen
Idea and planning Hubertus Gassner, Mario-A. von Lüttichau
General editors Karin Bellmann, Mario-A. von Lüttichau
Authors of commentary texts
Hubertus Gassner (HG), Hubertus Froning (Fro), Kathrin Kohle (K.K.), Ulrike Köcke (Kö), Christiane Kuhlmann (CK), Agnes Matthias (AM), Hella Nocke-Schrepper (HN), Diana Schmies (DS), Mario-A. von Lüttichau (vL), Petra Steinhardt (PS), Kyllikki Zacharias (KyZ).
Photographs Jens Nober
Cover illustrations
Rodin, *The Bronze Age*
Gauguin, *Barbarian Tales*
Serrano, *The Interpretation of Dreams (Black Santa)*

British Library Cataloguing-in-Publication Data: a catalogue record for this book is available from the British Library; Deutsche Bibliothek holds a record of this publication in the Deutsche Nationalbibliografie; detailed bibliographical data can be found under: http://dnb.ddb.de

© Prestel Verlag,
Munich · Berlin · London · New York, 2005

Prestel Verlag
Königinstrasse 9, 80539 Munich
Telephone: +49-(89) 38 17 09-0
Telefax: +49-(89) 38 17 09-35
www.prestel.de

Prestel Publishing Ltd.
4, Bloomsbury Place, London WC1A 2QA
Telephone: +44 (020) 7323-5004
Telefax: +44 (020) 7636-8004

Prestel Publishing
900 Broadway, Suite 603, New York, NY 10003
Telephone: +1 (212) 995-2720
Telefax: +1 (212) 995-2733
www.prestel.com

Translated by Michael Robinson
Copy-edited by Paul Aston
Layout and production
a.visus, Michael Hempel, Munich
Repro Reproline Genceller, Munich
Printing and binding Passavia Druckservice GmbH, Passau
Printed on chlorine-free bleached paper

ISBN 3-7913-2994-4 (German edition)
ISBN 3-7913-2993-6 (English edition)

Picture credits

Information

Folkwang Museum, Essen

Goethestrasse 41
D-45128 Essen, Germany
Phone +49-[0]201-8845 314
Fax +49-[0]201-8845 001

Opening hours

Tuesday to Sunday 10 a.m. to 6 p.m.
Friday 10 a.m. to midnight

Closed:
New Year's Day, Easter Monday,
Whit Monday, 1st May, Christmas Eve
and New Year's Eve

Museum café & restaurant

Breakfast, lunch, wholefoods,
set menus, desserts, buffet,
snacks, coffee and cakes, cocktails,
wines
Phone +49-[0]201-7961 33
Open during museum opening hours

Folkwang-Museumsverein e.V.,

founded 1922 during the purchase of
Karl Ernst Osthaus's Hagen Folkwang
Collection, is responsible for and owner
of the Folkwang Museum collection,
jointly with the City of Essen.
Phone +49-[0]201-8845 002
Fax +49-[0]201-8845 001

Kunstring Folkwang e.V., founded in
1901 as a museum association, has
since that date organised lectures,
courses, guided tours and excursions,
concerts, film screenings, campaigns
and workshop discussions, and
provides information on current
Folkwang Museum exhibitions and
activities.
Phone +49-[0]201-7747 83
Fax +49-[0]201-7883 30
Open Tuesday to Friday from 10 a.m.
to 12 noon

The museum education service
follows the current exhibition programme and organises on request
guided tours on specific subjects for
school groups, children's painting
lessons and holiday projects for
children. The education service also
offers guided tours of the Museum
Folkwang Collection for adults.
Phone +49-[0]201-8845 301

The library carries specialist
literature, catalogues and magazines
on the Folkwang Museum's art
collections.
Phone +49-[0]201-8845 317
Open Tuesday 10 a.m. to 1 p.m.,
Thursday 10 a.m. to 1 p.m, 3 to 6 p.m..

Kindly supported by Nationalbank AG,
Essen.